CARLTON COSMO RICE (1876–1945)

UNIVERSITY OF NORTH CAROLINA
STUDIES IN THE ROMANCE LANGUAGES
AND LITERATURES

ROMANCE ETYMOLOGIES AND OTHER STUDIES

By

CARLTON COSMO RICE (1876-1945)

ARRANGED BY

Urban T. Holmes, Jr.

CHAPEL HILL

1946

Copyright, 1946
THE UNIVERSITY OF NORTH CAROLINA

CARLTON COSMO RICE

(1876–1945)

Professor Rice was born on August 12, 1876, at Paton, Iowa. As an undergraduate he attended the University of Texas where he received his bachelor's degree in 1897, and his master's two years later. Harvard University awarded him another M.A. in 1900, and he obtained his doctorate there in 1902. Dr. Rice was at Harvard University when the language departments were approaching the peak of their excellence. He studied Old French with E. S. Sheldon, Spanish and Early Portuguese with the young J. D. M. Ford, whose meteoric rise carried with it great enthusiasm for the languages of the Iberian Peninsula. He had courses in Italian and Provençal with C. H. Grandgent whose fame as a scholar and teacher were second to none. At Harvard Rice caught an enthusiasm which endured throughout his professional life.

Since 1926 when he first came to Catawba College, Professor Rice was active in modern language affairs in the southeastern section of the country. He was one of the founders of SAMLA. In 1928 he became affiliated with the Linguistic Society of America and he showed great devotion to this Society. He was nearly always present at the sessions of the Linguistic Institute. I can remember how in July 1929 I was motoring home from a brief vacation in Maine and stopped for a few hours at a boarding house close to the Yale University campus. When I mentioned to the landlady that I was headed south she remarked with enthusiasm, "Why there is a man here who drove all the way from North Carolina to attend the Linguistic Institute." It was Professor Rice. That was the first time I made his acquaintance, which was to be constantly renewed at many professional meetings.

During his early teaching days Rice was often troubled by illness. Perhaps this is the reason for the shyness which was so marked in his character, oddly enough in view of his mental vigor and curiosity. He taught first at Oregon, after receiving his Ph.D. He was there only a year when he was called to Stanford University. There, I have been told, he overworked to such an extent that he had to withdraw from teaching in 1905. He returned to the field in the University of Iowa (1907–9), and then moved to the University of Idaho (1909–11). While at Idaho he printed his doctoral dissertation on "The Phonology of Gallic Clerical Latin after the Sixth Century." An abstract of this had appeared in the *Journal Amer. Phil. Assoc.*, XXXV (1904), lxiv–lxv.

Reprinted from the *South Atlantic Bulletin* XI (Dec., 1945), 10–11.

In 1911 Professor Rice again withdrew from teaching, this time for a period of fifteen years. In 1914-17 he was employed at the Library of Congress. He was a translator with the Post Office Department during the first World War, and then he was with War Risk Insurance and the Red Cross. The increase in the Tariff Commission which came about under President Coolidge brought him to that bureau where he was engaged in making an index of foreign periodicals on commercial and economic subjects. At this juncture he accepted the call to Catawba College.

Perhaps it was due to the inspiration which had first come to him from Ford of Harvard that Professor Rice's first interest in research was in Spanish and Portuguese etymologies. He published a continuous series of these, mostly in the journal *Language*. Not all were accepted by his professional colleagues, but some found their way into Meyer-Lübke's *Romanisches Etymologisches Wörterbuch* (3rd. ed., 1935). In March 1930 (*Language* VI, 36-40) Rice published an etymology of Sanskrit *guṇa* 'bovine' which he had worked out in the Sanskrit seminar at the Linguistic Institute. Specially to be remembered is his interest in the Waldensian Colony at Valdese, N. C. In 1941 Professor Rice showed me the last work he had done on this subject, an edition of the Waldensian material which he had carefully copied from a text appearing in 1669. This has not been published. Professor Rice's major work on which he labored for many years is a *Glossary of Attested Semantic Changes*. When this was undertaken Rice did not know of a similar plan projected by Carl Buck of the University of Chicago. Professor Rice's materials are neatly filed on cards and it may be possible to continue with them. He had a strong urge to learn all languages. In 1937 he undertook to learn modern Breton and achieved considerable fluency in the written language.

I last saw Professor Rice at a meeting of a group interested in Renaissance literature which met at Chapel Hill in the winter of 1945. Although the subjects discussed were not directly in the field of his interest, Rice listened with great attention and made his contribution.

Professor Rice is survived by his wife, Mrs. Dora L. Rice, whom he married in March, 1944.

U. T. H., Jr.

PREFACE

In offering this collection of Professor Rice's etymologies and other studies no attempt has been made to modify the contents of the articles. This is a field in which authorities often differ and an arranger can not conscientiously alter something to suit his own tastes which may be directly contrary to the wishes of the author. Where Professor Rice left notes indicating a change of opinion this has been added.

It was our first plan to list the etymologies alphabetically. However, many of them are very short and this would have broken up the text into too many single paragraphs. It would have meant also an elaborate rearranging of the notes. Accordingly the etymological articles are placed in approximate chronological order, except that a subsequent article recording a change of opinion is placed directly after the first one to which it refers.

It was Professor Rice's own intention to collect his etymologies into a single volume. Mrs. Dora L. Rice wished to carry out this plan for him and she has made it possible for us to issue the volume in this present form. Permission to reprint material already published has been graciously granted by the present editors of the *Publications of the Modern Language Association, Modern Language Notes, Modern Philology, Hispanic Review, Modern Language Forum,* and *Language*. In referring to previous publication we have used the abbreviations *PMLA, MLN, MPhil, HR,* and *MLF*, respectively. *Language* is abbreviated to *Lang*.

U. T. H., Jr.

TABLE OF CONTENTS
ROMANCE ETYMOLOGIES

I. Old Spanish *consograr, consagrar, *consangrar* 3
II. Italian *gręggio, gręẓẓo* 7
III. Romance Words for "to go" 12
IV. Italian *andare; agio; malvagio* 23
V. *Anar-andare-aller* < *adnare-*annitare-*annulare* 27
VI. French *fléchir*; Spanish *rosca, sesgo*; French *ruche* 29
VII. Spanish *estragar; sesgar; simado; sosegar* 34
VIII. Additional Notes on Spanish *estragar, sesgar, simado, (sima), sosegar*... 38
IX. Spanish *bazo; cerdo; empachar; esquejar; estropear; estrujar* 41
X. Spanish *abarca; ciscar;* ¡*ole!* 46
XI. More on *ciscar* 48
XII. Provençal *escacha*; Italian *frizzare, paggio*; Old French *puirier*; Provençal *trobar* 50
XIII. Spanish *alarido*; Portuguese *atanar*; Spanish *cinchar*; Portuguese *deitar*; Spanish *dejar, pinchar* 53
XIV. More on Portuguese *deixar*; Spanish *dejar*; Sicilian *dassari* 58
XV. Spanish *columbrar* "to descry", *vislumbrar* "to see dimly" 60
XVI. Spanish *corral, loco,* and *mozo* 62
XVII. Provençal *avalir*; Portuguese *canhos*; Italian *goffo*; Catalan *migrarse*; Italian *mucca*; Modern Provençal *boutareu, poutarel, poutar* 64
XVIII. Spanish *bastar, despachar, rajar,* and *regunzar* 67
XIX. Old Spanish *regunçar* < **recomputiare* 70
XX. French *potiron* 72
XXI. Catalan *abaltir*; Italian *cansare*; Extremaduran Spanish *destorgar*; Catalan *enconar*; Spanish *lasca, regazar* 73
XXII. Spanish *halagar, nesga, socarrar* 76
XXIII. Spanish *chistar, rematar, sollo, tusa* 78
XXIV. Still more on *chistar, dejar, regunzar* 80
XXV. Spanish *quejarse*; Old Spanish *quexar* 82
XXVI. Lyonese *tona*; Spanish *espita*; Portuguese *rilhar* 84
XXVII. Portuguese *boroa, espirrar, fechar, paspalho, rosnar* 86
XXVIII. More on κάμψειν, Spanish *cansar* and on Greek etyma in Romance 88

OTHER STUDIES

XXIX. Sanskrit *guṇá* 93
XXX. Notes on the Present Status of the Catalan Language 97
XXXI. Close and open *e* and *o* at the Centro de Estudios Madrid 99
XXXII. The Standard of Correct Pronunciation of French in French Canada... 105
XXXIII. Close and open *e* and *o* in Cuba 114
XXXIV. The Accentuation of Spanish Verbs with Infinitive in *-iar* and *-uar* 119
XXXV. The Pronunciation of *e, o,* and *s* in Cultivated Italian 122
XXXVI. A Sketch of the Finistère Pronunciation of Literary Breton 129

Index of Words 135

ROMANCE ETYMOLOGIES

I

OLD SPANISH *CONSOGRAR*, *CONSAGRAR*, **CONSANGRAR*[1]

> Sed buenos mensageros, e ruego vos lo yo
> Que gelo digades albuen Campeador:
> Abra y ondra e creçra en onor,
> Por *conssagrar* con los yffantes de Carrion.
> *Poema del Çid*, 1903–6.

> Diego Gonçalez odredes lo que dixo:
> "De natura somos de los condes mas lipios,
> "Estos casamientos non fuessen apareçidos,
> "Por *consagrar* con myo Çid don Rodrigo."
> *Ibid.*, 3353–6.

The word *consagrar*, which occurs only in these two passages in the sense of 'to become related to by marriage,' has always puzzled the editors of the *Poema*, and has never yet, I believe, been correctly explained. In the early edition of T. A. Sanchez[2] we find *consograr* in both passages. F. Janer,[3] prints *conssagrar* in the first passage, with foot-note: "Con acierto Sanchez y Damas Hinard corrigen: *consograr*." In the second passage he writes *consograr*. A. Bello,[4] has *consograr* in both passages; in his glossary he defines the word thus:

"Consograr, emparentar con alguna persona, contrayendo matrimonio con hijo o hija suya, o dándole un hijo o hija en matrimonio, 1944, 3414, Alejandro 312."

Here it should be said that the exact nature of the relation entered into by the two kings in the *Alexandre*, stanza 312, to whom the expression *consogravan* is applied, is not apparent from the context; this passage cited by Bello can, therefore, prove nothing as to the force of the word in the *Cid*. E. Lidforss,[5] prints *conssograr*, *consograr*.

Now there are two serious objections to be urged against the reading *consograr*. In the first place, it involves a very improbable correction of

---

[1] In preparing these notes for publication I have profited much by the kind criticism of Prof. Sheldon.

[2] *Colección de poesías castellanas anteriores al siglo xv*, Vol. i, *Poema del Cid*, Madrid, 1779.

[3] *Biblioteca de autores españoles*, Vol. lvii, *Poetas castellanos anteriores, al siglo xv*, Madrid, 1864.

[4] *Obras completas*, Vol. ii, *El Poema del Cid*, Santiago de Chile, 1881. In this edition the lines are numbered 1944, 3414.

[5] *Los Cantares de Myo Cid*, Lund, 1895.

Reprinted from *MLN* XVI (1901), 236–38.

the unique manuscript. The text of Menéndez Pidal has *conssagrar*, *consagrar*, as quoted above; if there were the slightest doubt regarding the letter *a* in the codex, the editor in question would certainly have mentioned the fact. And it is very hard to believe that the scribe has erred twice in writing this rare and peculiar expression. In the second place, the reading *consograr* does not give the right meaning. In the poem, when the Infantes of Carrion marry the Cid's daughters, the relation into which the Infantes and the Cid enter with regard to each other is described by the verb *Consagrar*. *Consograr*, on the other hand, means "durch Verheiratung der *beiderseitigen* Kinder *Gegen*schwiegerältern werden."[6] The extension of the signification of *consocerum* in its Roumanian derivatives will certainly not be taken as an indication that the same phenomenon occurred in early Spanish.

Consograr is said by A. Restori[7] to be derived from *cum+socerari* (given without asterisk). I do not find *socerari* in Du Cange nor in the index to the *Corpus Glossariorum Latinorum*, and I am inclined to question its existence. At any rate, the best ultimate starting-point for the derivation of *consograr* is certainly *consocerum*, which is a well-attested Latin word. G. Körting[8] gives only the Roumanian descendant of *consocerum*, to which might be added Italian *consuocero*, and Spanish *consuegro*, Portuguese *consogro*, with the verbs formed therefrom (or possibly derived from an Iberian Latin **consocerare*).

A. Restori prints the reading *conssagrar*, *consagrar* in the passages under discussion, and derives the form from "*cum + sacrare da sacrum.*"[9] Later on it will be shown that the *consagrar* of our text is not, as Restori thinks, identical with the modern *consagrar*, the formation of which will be discussed now. Körting, mentioning the French *consacrer* as a derivative of *consacrare*, which he unnecessarily marks with an asterisk, says: "In den übrigen Sprachen ist *consecrare* als gelehrtes Wort vorhanden." The Romance forms of *consecrare* present certain difficulties which seem to deserve further explanation. The forms which I have noted are early Italian *consagrare*, Spanish, Catalan, Portuguese and Old Provençal *consagrar*, Old Catalan *consegrar*, Italian *consacrare*, Modern Provençal *consacra*, Old and Modern French *consacrer*, Old French *consecrer*. It will be observed that, if sound-development were taken into consideration alone, the first two forms given would have to be called popular, since they present the vulgar vowel *a* in the root-syllable and have also suffered the popular

[6] Tolhausen, *Wörterbuch*, s. v.
[7] *Le Gesta del Cid*, 1890, p. 219.
[8] *Lateinisch-romanisches Wörterbuch*, Panderborn, 1901.
[9] *L. c.*, p. 219. The formula is, of course, inaccurate, since the word goes back directly to *consacrare*.

development of intervocalic *cr* to *gr*. The same may be said of the Old Catalan *consegrar*, which at first sight seems to show a learned retention of the *e* in *consecrare*, but which, according to H. Suchier,[10] merely furnishes an example of the confusion, regular in Old Catalan, of *a* and *e* before the accent. Still, in spite of these correct developments, it would scarcely be justifiable to infer that *consecrare* remained in popular use in some localities from the earliest times to the period when the Romance literatures made their appearance. The meaning of the word, on the contrary, seems to mark it as one of those numerous clerkly expressions associated with the services of the Church, which kept finding their way into the popular speech for several centuries after the acceptance of Christianity in Romance countries. Assuming, then, as Körting seems to do, that all the forms of *consecrare* in Romance were borrowed from the literary language, and not handed down from antiquity by oral tradition, how are we to account for the seemingly *popular* developments which they present? The vowel *a* of the root-syllable surely points to an ecclesiastical Latin pronunciation of *consecrare* with *a* instead of *e* in the second syllable, the rule observed by the vernacular in the pronunciation of recognized compounds of being followed, during a certain period, by the learned language as well. The development of intervocalic *cr* to *gr* might lead one to suppose that the word became popular before the sixth century, at which time, at least in Gaul, this sound-change probably took place. But this does not necessarily follow, since the learned language in the early middle ages was affected by many of the vulgar consonant-developments. All the forms with *gr* may accordingly go back to the clerical *consagrare*, which existed in Gaul in the seventh, probably even in the sixth century. The date of the popularization of the word in Gaul, and probably in Spain, is earlier than that of the introduction of French *consacrer*, Provençal *consacra* (showing partial correction), which doubtless occurred after the third quarter of the eighth century. In like manner, Italian *consacrare* is a later correction of *consagrare*. The French *consecrer*, another late learned affectation, did not succeed in replacing *consacrer*, and went out of use.

Restori is undoubtedly right in preferring the reading of the MS. to the emendation *consograr*, but his identification of the *consagrar* of our text with the modern Spanish *consagrar* is open to serious objection. It is surely improbable that an expression meaning literally 'to consecrate' should have acquired in these two passages, and nowhere else, the meaning *to become related by marriage*. It should be especially noticed that *consacrare* (*consecrare*) and its modern derivatives are *transitive;* and I have been unable, after patient search, to find any evidence for a similar change in the construction and signification of *consecrare* (*consacrare*) anywhere,

[10] *Dkm. prov. Lit. u. Spr.*, 1883, p. 564.

either in Latin or in Romance. Considering the religious character of the marriage ceremony, it is of course not impossible to imagine that the expression to *consecrate* [*the bond of wedlock*] *with one* should have developed to express the idea *to become related by marriage to one*. But until some unquestionable evidence can be produced for this remarkable transfer of meaning, it must be considered highly improbable. Indeed it was precisely this semasiological difficulty that caused the editors to approve almost unanimously the emendation *consograr* above discussed.

Since both these explanations of our text are clearly unsatisfactory, I have ventured, in the Old Spanish Seminary at Harvard conducted by Dr. J. D. M. Ford, to present a new one. I propose to derive the MS. form *consagrar*—if this form be accepted—from **consanguinare*. This gives exactly the right meaning, namely; *to consanguinate with*.[11] The formation of **consanguinare* in Latin is as natural as that of **consangrar* in Spanish; cf. *illuminare, exstirpare*, etc., compounds formed directly from substantive stems. I have no direct proof of the existence of the word, although Du Cange quotes *consanguinitare* from a glossary, where it is defined as signifying *sanguini* [for sanguine?] *propinquitare*. **Consanguinare* should give, according to phonetic laws, *consangnar*, later *consangrar*. The loss of the second *n* in our text may conceivably be due to dissimilation, or to the influence of *consagrar* < *consacrare*. I would call attention, however, to the carelessness with which the letters *m* and *n* (very often represented only by a nasal dash over the preceding vowel) are used in the unique manuscript of the *Poema del Çid*. The following examples, taken from Menéndez Pidal's edition, will illustrate this point:[12] *etro* for *entro* (47), *Marti* for *Martin* (141 ‡), *pagava* for *pagavan* (186 ‡), *mebrados* for *membrados* (315 ‡), *etrar* for *entrar* (665 ‡), *destellado* for *destellando* (762), *laças* for *lanças* (834 ‡), *desaparaua* for *desemparaua* (910 ‡), *ded* for *dend* (1063 ‡, 2134), *dozitos* for *dozientos* (1164), *ale* for *alen* (1896), *era* for *eran* (2267 ‡), *capo* for *campo* (2343), *tatas* for *tantas* (2400 ‡), *ebayr* for *embayr* (3011), *ondrasse* for *ondrassen* (3155 ‡), *relumbra* for *relumbran* (3177 ‡), *lipios* for *limpios* (3354), *veçido* for *vençido* (3484 ‡). The omission of the nasal dash before a consonant being common in the codex, I suggest that we should restore **consangrar* in both the passages quoted above. Accepting this form, we may quite readily explain it as a Romance development (*con*+*sangre*+*ar*), and the existence of a Latin **consanguinare*, though of course still quite possible, may be doubted.

[11] For the English word, see Murray's *Dictionary*.
[12] The ‡ indicates that the missing nasal dash was inserted later by a corrector.

II

ITALIAN *GRĘGGIO, GREŻŻO*

The most recent detailed study of the Italian word appearing in the forms *gręggio* and *grężżo* is D'Ovidio's extended discussion in *Romania*, Vol. XXV, pp. 295 ff. This scholar agrees with Fumi[1] in rejecting the etymon *agrestis*[2] suggested by Caix[3] and likewise the type **gregius* set up by Canello.[4] The etymon **ἄγροικος* [!] proposed by Roensch[5] appears never to have been taken very seriously. The type which D'Ovidio accepts as the probable etymon, namely **grĕvius*, was first suggested by Fumi, who, however, was not able to explain the phonetic irregularities which the assumption of such an etymon involves. D'Ovidio attempts to overcome the difficulties by assuming that the word came into Tuscan from Venetian territory. According to him, by the side of **levius* (> *leggio*) for *levis*, a form **grĕvius* for **grevis* may have existed in colloquial Latin. Then just as *pluvia* gave in Venetian *pioza* (nowadays *piova*), so **grĕvius* may have given **grezo*. The *e* in this word would probably have been close, according to D'Ovidio, as in Venetian *greve* and *me greva*. The meaning of *gręggio, grężżo* is "rough, unworked." Since, during the Middle Ages, the Venetians excelled in the various arts, it is possible that this word **grezo* came into common use among them as a technical term and was borrowed as such by Tuscans. Assuming this introduction of the word into Tuscany, it may also be assumed, according to D'Ovidio, that some Tuscans would accept **grezo* in the form *grężżo*, while others would substitute for the Venetian *z* the group which usually represents this Venetian sound in Tuscan, *i.e.*, *ġġ* (cf. Venetian *mazor, pezo*, etc.).

This etymon **grevius* is the only one thus far proposed meriting serious consideration now, since *agrestis* and **gregius* have already been disposed by Paris and Fumi.[6] Now, *grĕvius*, notwithstanding D'Ovidio's argumentation, still presents great difficulties. In the first place, we may, of course, doubt whether the word ever existed; but admitting the possibility of its existence, it may again be doubted whether it would have developed

---

[1] *Misc. Caix-Canello*, pp. 99 ff.

[2] This etymon is also rejected by Paris (Romania, Vol. VIII, p. 618).

[3] *Studia di etimologia italiana e romanza*, § 39.

[4] *Archivio glottologico*, Vol. III, p. 348.

[5] *Rom. Forsch.*, Vol. III, p. 372.

[6] The etymon *gregeos* (Old French), suggested by Petrocchi in his *Dizionario scolastico*, presents insuperable phonetic difficulties.

Reprinted from *MPhil* I (1903), 337–42.

into *grezo in the dialect of Venice, since D'Ovidio gives only one word showing the development vy > z, and in that very case the modern dialect shows not z, but v. Admitting, however, again that in this assumed word the development vy > z may actually have taken place in Venice, it is difficult to suppose that the word passed from Venetian into Tuscan in both Venetian and Tuscanized form, so as to give both grẹżżo and grẹggio in Tuscan. For this last assumption not a single parallel is cited. And, above all, why go to Venice to find an explanation for word-forms which, according to all manifest probabilities, originated in Tuscany? Taken all together, these objections are certainly serious. D'Ovidio, it should be said, is quite aware of the weak points in his theory, and claims only to have established a probability in favor of *grĕvius. Körting, who discusses the Fumi-D'Ovidio theory under the word *agrestis*,[7] reaches the following result: "Aber auch Fumi's annahme hat keineswegs die wahrscheinlichkeit für sich, und die ableitung des wortes muss also noch fraglich bezeichnet werden, wie das schon Diez 377 gethan hatte."

It is thus quite in place to suggest a new etymon. Thus far etymologists, taking the meaning of the Italian word as their starting-point, have looked for an etymon meaning something like "rough." Having found or invented an ancient word giving approximately the right meaning, they have been constrained to assume an unparalleled development of one or another consonant-group in order to explain the phonetic relation of the Italian word to the etymon proposed. I believe that a start taken from the form of the Italian word leads to better results. The consonants żż beside ġġ almost certainly presuppose an ancient word in dy (cf. rażżo beside *raggio* < *radium*, *mężżo* < *medium*, *rożżo* < **rudium*, beside *moggio* < *modium*, *poggio* < *podium*, etc.). No other combination unquestionably giving both ġġ and żż in Tuscan has ever been cited. We should certainly look first of all for an ancient *grẹdius, the development of which into both *grẹggio* and *grẹżżo* would not present the slightest phonetic difficulty. Now *grẹdius is not attested, but a very near neighbor, namely *gęrdius*, is found. It occurs in Lucilius apud Nonium Marcellum 118, 10, and in Julius Firmicus Maternus 8, 25 *med*. This word *gerdius*, which is given as meaning "weaver," is the Latin form of the Greek γέρδιος. The citation from Lucilius points to a very early borrowing, so that we are obliged to assume that the e of the Latin word was close, as was the Greek ε in early times. The passage from *gęrdius* to **grẹdius* of course offers a slight difficulty, but is rendered probable enough by parallels such as Provençal *tresol* beside *tersol* < *tertiolus*, Italian *troppo*, French *trop*, probably going back to *porp*, Italian dialectic *trevetino* beside *tevertino* < *tiburtinus*, Old French *troubler* beside *tourbler* < *turbulare*, Old French *trousseau*

---

[7] The Italian words are missing in Körting's index.

beside *torseau*, Italian *torsello*, French *treuil* beside Italian *torchio* < *torculum*, Spanish *trujal* < *torcular*. I cite these few examples from Körting and refer for others to Meyer-Lübke,[8] who expressly remarks: "Namentlich stark ausgeprägt ist die tendenz *r* mit dem anlautenden konsonanten zu verbinden." The closest parallel among the examples cited by Meyer-Lübke is that of *crovus* for *corvus*, occurring in western upper Italy and in Sicily. I have not been able to find any parallel showing an *r* passing over to an initial *g*; but this is not surprising in view of the fact that the number of words presenting an initial *g* followed by vowel + *r* is comparatively small. Moreover, parallels of this type, if existing, would be etymologically obscure on account of the metathesis, and for that reason could not readily be located. A possible physiological cause for the shift from *gẹrdius* to **grẹdius* is not far to seek: when nonsyllabic *i* became *y*, the group *ẹrdy* was doubtless unique and difficult to pronounce, so that the shift to the easily articulated *grẹdy* might well be expected.

I now turn to the semasiological development of *gerdius*. Since, as has been said, the Latin word is attested twice apparently in the meaning of "weaver," while the Italian word is an adjective meaning "rough, unworked," the shift in sense which must be assumed appears to present considerable difficulty. A reference to the dictionary shows, however, that the Italian word is commonly used in phrases which immediately suggest an ancient connection in sense with a word meaning something like "weaver." Petrocchi's article on the Italian word reads as follows:

Grèggio,[9] *grẹżżo*, aggettivo. La materia delle diverse arti prima che sia lavorata. Come sono estratti dalle miniere. *Legno, Lana, Lino, Canapa gregge:* prima che sian lavorate. *Seta greggia:* adoprata come esce dalla filanda e collo stesso colore. *Tela greggia:* di lino grigiastra, piuttosto ruvida. *Ragazzi, Animi, Menti greggi:* non ancora educati, istruiti.

It is quite easy to derive all these meanings from the fundamental notion of "pertaining to the weaver." We have only to postulate the series: (1) "weaver's," (2) "fresh-woven," (3) "rough and untrimmed" (of cloth), (4) "rough and unworked" (of other materials). If Forcellini is right in assuming that the Latin word meant "carder" rather than "weaver," we may modify the scheme as follows: (1) "carder's," (2) "for the carder," i.e., "rough" (of the various materials which are carded, such as wool, flax, etc.), (3) "rough, unworked" (of other materials like silk, wood, minerals). The only point presenting difficulty is the shift from the value

[8] *Rom. Gram.*, Vol. I, p. 481.
[9] Petrocchi is certainly wrong in marking the *e* of *greggio* as open, since D'Ovidio (article cited, p. 296) states that "(*grẹggio*) ha l'*ẹ* in tutta Toscana e su ogni labbro italiano che non sia inetto a distinguere i du suoni dell'*e*."

"Weaver" or "carder" to the value "weaver's" or "carder's." We might perhaps assume that the noun gręggio = "weaver" or "carder," going out of use in prehistoric Italian except in phrases like *tela a gręggio* or *lana a gręggio*, phonetically *tęlaggręġġo, lanaggręġġo*, came to be felt as an adjective, whence *tela gręggia, lana gręggia*. It seems probable, however, that the adjectival use of Italian *gręggio* has a more ancient origin, going back to an adjectival use of the Greek and Latin words. The etymology and original meaning of γέρδιος are not apparent, but Du Cange cites a gloss defining it with the words ὑφάντρια, ὑφαντής, proving that it was feminine as well as masculine. It thus shows resemblance in form to the class of adjectives which may be declined with either two or three endings. Moreover, the collateral forms γερδιός, γερδαῖος, γερδεῖος must constitute with γέρδιος an adjectival group. Adjective doublets like ἄγριος and ἀγρεῖος from ἄγρος, Βάκχειος (Βακχεῖος) and Βάκχιος from Βάκχος, δούλιος and δούλειος from δοῦλος, θαλάσσιος and θαλασσαῖος from θάλασσα, may be seen on every other page of the lexicon, and even triplets like λοχεῖος, λοχαῖος, and λόχιος from λόχος, νυμφεῖος, νυμφαῖος, and νύμφιος from νύμφη, are not extremely uncommon. Since a similar formation of original nouns is out of the question, we must place the group γέρδιος, γερδιός, γερδεῖος, γερδαῖος in the same category, in spite of the fact that they are attested as substantives only. It is thus clear that γέρδιος—meagerly attested in both Greek and Latin in the meaning of "weaver," was originally an adjective (meaning[10] probably "pertaining to the web," or "pertaining to the card");

[10] Forms of γέρδιος are not given by the ordinary lexicons; they occur almost exclusively in glosses. The forms given in Hesychius and Suidas, in Sophocles's *Greek Lexicon of the Roman and Byzantine Periods*, in the *Middle Latin* and *Middle Greek Lexicons* of Du Cange, in the *Corpus Glossariorum Latinorum*, in Johannes Meursius's *Lexicon Graeco-barbarum* (Greek-Latin dictionary, Lugduni Batavorum, anno CIƆ.IC·C.XIV.), and in Stephanus's *Thesaurus Graecae Linguae*, which have been sent to me by my friends Dr. J. C. Watson, of Cornell University, and Mr. E. Cary, Fellow in Harvard University, are as follows: γέρδης, γέρδιος, γερδιός, γερδαῖος, γερδεῖος, all defined as meaning ὑφάντης, *textor;* γέρδιος = ὑφάντρια, ὑφαντής; γερδία = *textrix;* γερδίσαι = *textrices;* γερδοποιόν (for γερδοποιεῖον?) = *textrinum;* συγγέρδιαι = συνυφάντριαι; γερδιακός. With regard to the etymology of γέρδιος, Stephanus notes: "Secundum Schneid. est ab Aeolico ἔρδω pro ἔργω;" but this derivation is obviously objectionable. Forcellini *s. v.* says: "Ipsa certe vox peregrina est: videtur enim esse a Chald. *garday* quod vulgo vertitur *textor;* sed cum Hebr. *garad* significet *decorticavit*, vero [*sic!*] simile est interpretandum esse carminatorem, Italice *cardatore*, a carduis nempe quibus in carminando utitur." This view of the origin of γέρδιος is mentioned and rejected by the editor of the *Thesaurus Syriacus*, who accepts the derivation of the Semitic group from the Greek. The Semitic forms, for which I am indebted to Mr. Cary, are as follows: Chaldaic *garday* = "weaver;" Hebrew *garod* = "*decorticavit*" (ἅπαξ λελεγμένον occurring in the Book of Job); Syriac *gardā'* = "*glaber, tela, textura, iugum textoris* (loom-beam)," *gardyāyā'* = "*textor*," *grad* = "*erasit. scalpsit, delevit;*" Modern Syriac *jrādā* = "carpet woven on a frame," *jerdî* = "the

and it may have remained long in use in this adjectival sense in both ancient languages. The postulation of the coexistence of the assumed adjectival value with the attested substantival value presents no difficulty: cf. μουσικός, "musical" and also "scholar;" and *consularis*, "pertaining to the consul" and also "ex-consul." Similar parallels might be cited in great abundance from both Greek and Latin.

Summing up, it may be said that phonetic law unequivocally requires the etymon *grędius, the derivation of which from *gerdius* = γέρδιος presents virtually no phonetic difficulty. A semasiological obstacle is the circumstance that the ancient word is attested as a substantive only, while the Italian word is an adjective. In view of the fact, however, that the ancient word is of rare occurrence in both Latin and Greek, while the Greek word is shown by its formation to have been originally, at least, an adjective, the assumption of an adjectival value for the Greek-Latin substratum certainly seems to be justified. But whether the apparent shift from the value of "weaver" to that of "weaver's" should be explained in this or in some other way, the assumed change of function is, after all, hardly violent enough to present material difficulty.

---

frame for weaving carpets" and "the carpets themselves." (Lexicons: J. Levy, *Chaldäisches Wörterbuch, etc.*, Leipzig, 1867; *Thesaurus Syriacus* .... edidit R. P. Smith, Oxford, 1879; J. Brun, *Dictionarium Syriaco-Latinum, Beryti Phoeniciorum*, 1895; A. J. Maclean, *A Dictionary of Vernacular Syriac, etc.*, Oxford, 1901.) Whatever be the ultimate relation of the Greek to the Semitic group, it is clear that the attested Greek secondary forms must be derived from primary forms which went out of use or accidentally escaped registration. The gloss γερδοποιόν = *textrinum*, which has been emended to γερδοποιεῖον = *textrinum* (the Latin word being used in the sense of *textrina*, as elsewhere), however it be taken, seems to presuppose a primary word *γερδος meaning "web." The Syriac *gardā'* = *tela* also deserves notice. On the other hand, Lucilius, as Meursius (*s. v.*) pointed out, differentiates *textor* and *gerdius* in the passage: "curate domi sint Gerdius ancillae pueri zonarius textor." This, of course, supports Forcellini's view that *gerdius* meant "carder." Possibly we should also assume a word *γερδη = "card," "teasel," from which all the forms except γερδοποιόν may be derived. One might be tempted to identify the base of γέρδιος with that of κείρω, "to clip." Note that the latter is supposed to be cognate with Latin *caro*, "to card;" *carduus*, "thistle." For the γ, cf. γαμψός from κάμπτω. At all hazards, it is probable that γέρδιος meant originally "pertaining to the web" or "pertaining to the card." The difference between these values and "pertaining to the weaver," "pertaining to the carder," is so slight that it may be overlooked, particularly since the sense of the Italian word may be readily derived from either member of either pair.

III

ROMANCE WORDS FOR "TO GO"

In dem Abschnitt über die romanischen Sprachen welchen die "Année linguistique" Bd. I (1901-1902) enthält, widmet A. Dauzat auch den Etymologieen ein paar kurze und abgerissene Bemerkungen und preist dabei den "scepticisme salutaire" den Gaston Paris in Bezug auf das Problem *aller-andare* an den Tag gelegt hat (S. 33). Dieser Skeptizismus ist keineswegs heilsam gewesen. Gegen zwei Erkenntnisse, welche, längst vorbereitet, jetzt fast Gemeingut geworden sind, hat sich G. P. bis zuletzt gesträubt und dadurch unter den Seinigen dem Aufkommen neuer phantastischer Erklärungen Vorschub geleistet. Diese Erkenntnisse sind: dass nur *ambulare* (mit oder ohne *ambitare als Variante) das Grundwort für jene romanischen Verben sein kann, und ferner dass diese—sogar auch dann wenn für sie ein anderer Ursprung vorauszusetzen wäre—auf ganz regelmässige Weise sich nicht haben entwickeln können. Bei seiner Kritik jener Aufstellung hat G. P. Bedeutung und Gebrauchsumfang der Wörter nicht hinlänglich gewürdigt—dachte er doch selbst, auch für *aller*, an ein *addare = addere gradum*, und hat diesen Gedanken wohl nie ganz aufgegeben (s. z. B. Rom. XXVII, 627). Hinsichtlich des zweiten Punktes ist zu bemerken dass wir über das Wie? noch sehr verschiedene Ansichten hegen, aber keiner von uns die seinige für unwiderleglich halten dürfte. Da wir nun selbst die im Wege stehenden Schwierigkeiten nicht verkennen, so hatte es G. P. leicht jede einzelne Ansicht zu beanstanden, wobei er sich aber manchmal gar zu dogmatisch äusserte (ich verstehe z. B. nicht warum er Rom. XXXI, 607 das Wulffsche Δ nicht sonderbar findet, wohl aber *ambitare neben *ambulare*, trotz lat.-rom. Verben wie *miscitare* neben *misculare*, *circitare* neben *circulare*, *tremitare* neben *tremulare*, *crepitare* neben *crepulare* u. s. w.); in Ganzen hat er hier doch nur, freilich ohne es zu wollen, die Rolle eines advocatus diaboli gespielt. Das Unregelmässige dessen Annahme hier unvermeidlich ist, bedeutet nicht etwas was im Widerspruch zu andern Tatsachen der Sprache stünde, sondern nur etwas was sich nicht in eine Tatsachengruppe einordnen lässt; eine Sprache deren Entwicklung keine solche Unregelmässigkeiten aufwiese, wäre das Allerunregelmässigste, sie ist geradezu undenkbar. Man verkennt gar zu leicht den gesellschaftlichen Character der Sprache; man vergegenwärtigt sich nicht hinlänglich dass auch der anscheinend einfachste sprachliche Vorgang in Wirklichkeit ein sehr verwickelter ist, und dass eine ganz geringfügige Abänderung eines seiner Faktoren genügt haben könnte um ihn nicht eintreten zu lassen. Wenn wir in der Wissenschaft immer das Einfachere suchen, so tun wir es indem wir in die Höhe streben. Es wäre aber ein Irrtum überall, auch in der Niederung, das Einfache finden zu wollen; "l'esprit simpliste n'est pas l'esprit scientifique." Es ist nicht bedeutungslos dass das ein Franzose—S. Reinach—gesagt hat, denn gerade bei den Franzosen ist der simplistische Geist sehr verbreitet. Er entstammt einer Tugend, dem Drang nach Klarheit und Bestimmtheit; "das tut man" oder "das tut man nicht," damit haben die Franzosen bei sich und auch bei andern Völkern erzieherisch gewirkt. Sobald wir aber die Schwelle der reinen Erkenntnis überschreiten, dürfen wir uns über die Dinge nicht bestimmter äussern als sie selbst es gestatten, sie nicht klarer sehen wollen als sie es sind. Aber wir

---

Reprinted from *PMLA* XIX (1904), 217-33.

dürfen auch nicht zu wenig tun. Wenn Dauzat sagt dass das *aller-andare*-Problem dank G. P. "intacte" bleibe, so ist das nicht richtig; wir werden vielleicht vergeblich auf eine Überraschung warten wie sie uns die Trümmerfelder des Morgenlandes nicht selten bescheren, und es wird uns somit vielleicht eine vollständige Lösung des Problems versagt bleiben (sicherlich eine welche "s'impose"; s. Rom. a. a. O.), aber eine halbe Lösung haben wir doch erreicht. Wenn der Maler uns eine Landschaft im nächtlichen Dunkel, in der Morgendämmerung, im Tagesschatten, im hellen Sonnenschein darstellen kann, so auch der Gelehrte irgend eine wissenschaftliche Frage— und sei es die nach dem Ursprung der Sprache—in demjenigen Stadium in dem sie sich gerade befindet. (*Zeitschrift für romanische Philologie*, 1904, pp. 52 f.)

This important discussion, from Schuchardt's pen, is quoted at some length here for the purpose of indicating with precision the status of the so-called *ambulare* question. It may be said at once that the writer of the present article belongs to the small group of phonologists still living who are not yet fully convinced that *aller* and *andare* must be derived from *ambulare*, and that the phonetic development of these verbs must necessarily have been irregular. The forms assuredly do appear to contain the same stem; but the precise character of this stem is an important matter which, in the opinion of the writer, still requires considerable elucidation. From the favorable reception accorded by Rydberg[1] to E. Bovet's recent monogenetic achievement bearing the title *Ancora il problema andare*, one might infer that, after the numerous discussions of the stem of *andare*, this scholar had really made interesting progress. On reading the account of his theory presented on pages 152 ff. of G. Stucke's dissertation entitled *Französisch aller und seine romanischen Verwandten*, we are very much disappointed. It turns out that in order to develop the Romance forms neatly from *ambulare*, Bovet introduces a new application of the well-known and still unexplained symbol △, which disposes of two or three refractory letters in a wonderfully mystifying fashion. Now, if a competent etymologist finds it necessary to contrive phonology of this mediocre type in order to bolster the claims of *ambulare*, is it not time to pause and ask whether, after all, *ambulare* is precisely the word we are all looking for? The △ hypothesis was, to be sure, a useful and original invention in its time; but Schuchardt has intimated more than once that it cannot be justly pronounced a whit more probable than any of the dozen other *ambulare* schemes. If it really were perfectly clear that *ambulare* presents the only possible starting-point for the development of

---

[1] *Jahresbericht über die Fortschritte der rom. Phil.*, VI. (1903), I., p. 292. "Eine vortreffliche Übersicht über die in älterer Zeit wie von späteren Forschern gemachten Vorschläge zur Erklärung der Entwicklung [von *aller* etc.] enthält E. Bovet's Arbeit *Ancora il problema andare*, die dem Ref. geeignet erscheint die Überzeugung zu befestigen, dass einzig und allein *ambulare* die Grundform zu *aller, andar* etc. sein kann."

the Romance verbs, a new application of the △ theory or any other good *ambulare* theory would certainly be most welcome. But let us consider the evidence by which the unique character of this etymon has been established. In the *Zeitschrift für romanische Philologie* for 1902, pp. 393 f., Schuchardt writes as follows:—

> In ähnlicher Weise ist Thomas an die *ambulare*-Masse herangetreten. Er sagt [*Mélanges étymologiques*, s. v. *anar*] dass alle diejenigen welche sich bemühen *aller*, *andare* u. s. w. auf eine gemeinsame Quelle zurück-zuführen, ihre Ohren den Lehren der Phonetik verschliessen, welche uns zurufe: "Jedes für sich!" Das ist ein etwas husarenmässiges Divide et impera. Ich weiss nicht wie die Polygenetiker sich die Sache vorstellen. Etwa in folgender Weise? Die Romanen, oder wenn man will, die Römer, hatten ein Verb *ambulare* von stattlicher, dauerhafter Leibesbeschaffenheit. Im Laufe der Jahrhunderte brauchten sie es beim Lateinschreiben mehr und mehr; dafür kam es in der Umgangssprache mehr und mehr ab und starb endlich aus. Zum Ersatz zog man aus den verstecktesten Winkeln des Sprachschatzes Verben hervor deren Bedeutung von der des Gehens mehr oder weniger entfernt war, und zwar wählte jede Hauptprovinz ein anderes Verb; nur hatten sie vorher untereinander ausgemacht dass es ein Verb auf *are* sein, dass es auf *a* anlauten, und dass darauf ein *l* oder *n* folgen müsste, offenbar in der Absicht die Gelehrten des 19. and 20. Jhts. auf den thörichten Gedanken zu bringen dass es sich um Fortsetzungen von *ambulare* handle. Im Ernste brauche ich hier die monogenetische Ansicht nicht zu verteidigen; das ist zum so und so vielten Male und in besonders nachdrücklicher Weise von E. Bovet in dem mir soeben zugesandten Aufsatze "Ancora il problema *andare*" geschehen. Im Einzelnen wird man sich wohl nicht sofort einigen. So muss ich gestehen dass wie sehr ich auch F. Wulff als Phonetiker schätze, seine lautgeschichtliche Entwicklung von *ambulare* mir ganz unwahrscheinlich ist; ja, da er selbst auf jede Begründung verzichtet, so verstehe ich nicht einmal wie wir uns das allerortige Einspringen des Tausendkünstlers △ für *l* zu denken haben. Ich war sehr überrascht als ich die Anmerkung von G. Paris dazu las, in der er dem Wulffschen Stammbaum den Preis zuerkennt; vielleicht hat ihn gerade die dogmatische Kürze bestochen. Man sollte meinen dass die Annahme einer Suffix-vertauschung bei *ambulare*, wie eine vermittelnde Ansicht, den Polygenetikern noch am ehesten zusagen würde; was Bovet dagegen vorbringt, scheint mir nicht schwer ins Gewicht zu fallen, darüber wird noch bei andern Gelegenheiten zu reden sein. Thomas bekümmert sich nach dem von ihm ausgesprochenen Grundsatze nicht um die andern romanischen Verben, sondern nur um prov. *anar*. Man glaubte schon längst die Pandorabüchse geleert, bis auf die trügerische Hoffnung, und immer neue Etymologieen entflattern ihr jetzt. *Anar* soll auf *annare*, "das Jahr durchleben" zurückgehen, das in einer altlateinischen Gebetformel bezeugt wird. Das prov. *desanar* wird nicht falsch, aber doch willkürlich mit "cesser de vivre" übersetzt, um daraus ein *anar* mit der Bedeutung "leben" abzuziehen; es ist nichts Anderes als *abire*, *exire*, *decedere*, *discedere*, *excedere*, *egredi* (meist auch ohne *de* oder *e vita*), (*mit dem Tode*) *abgehen* u. s. w. . . . Nun hoffe ich aber dass Thomas wenigstens konsequent sein und wie *anar* auf *annare*, so auch *aller* auf **allare* oder **alare* (ich empfehle das port. *alar*, das auch "flattern" bedeutet, hierbei zur Berücksichtigung) zurückführen wird, da ja nur diese beiden Formen den Ansprüchen der Phonetik, wie er sie gelten lässt, genügen.

This spirited criticism of the polygenetic theory is, I believe, thoroughly sound, as a mere defense of monogenesis; but it certainly does not seem to follow that *aller, anar* and *andare* are necessarily derived somehow from *ambulare*. I believe that Schuchardt and other authorities who impatiently insist that this word is unquestionably the right etymon, go a step too far, overlooking various other possibilities which should be considered. They apparently leave out of account, for instance, other etyma already discovered, of which there is a plentiful supply. Stucke estimates that there were already thirty-odd on hand—Latin, Greek, Germanic, Celtic, Arabic and Sanskrit—when he was writing page 15 of his dissertation (*i.e.*, probably about January, 1902). Passing over more recent finds, for the sake of argument, I should like to ask whether all these specimens, some of which ought to be good etyma, must be rejected without more ado because the Romans had a verb in *are* meaning "to walk," a word of majestic, durable form, beginning with *a* and containing an *l*. In the famous plea for monogenesis, Schuchardt also appeals to an *n*; but we do not find this important letter in *ambulare*. Under these circumstances, is it not admissible to agree with Stucke (p. VI), who believes that the etymology of the Romance words for "to go" is still enveloped in a certain obscurity (*ein gewisses Dunkel*)?

It has been said that Istrian *âmna* and Rhætian *amna* go back to Latin **amminare*, a form to be derived (in an unprecedented manner) from **ammulare*, which should somehow stand for *ambulare*, because, for some obscure reason, it ought not to be separated from Roumanian *umbla* "to walk," which is certainly derived from the popular etymon. The phonological difficulties presented by this etymology are obvious, and have of course already been noticed. Other solutions of the problem have been presented, but the obscurities remain. It is no wonder that none of the various lines between *ambulare* and **amminare* has become popular: there is no safe route. The forms represent different Latin words. If the Romance words do go back to **amminare*, as is often assumed (and do not presuppose a type **aminare*), this word is none other than Latin **adminare*, "to drive to," the existence of which is rendered certain by French *amener* "to bring." The semantic series (1) "to drive to," "to chase to," *zujagen* (transitive), (2) "to chase to," *zujagen* (intransitive), "to go hastily to," (3) "to go to," (4) "to go," presents no difficulty. It has never been demonstrated in a clear and simple manner that Latin verbs must have a remarkable phonetic history as soon as they develop the meaning "to go." It has never been proved, for instance, that Rhætian *ma*, which Diez identifies with *meare*, "to go," is or can be the same word as Rhætian *ala, la*, which are so often connected in an extremely irregular manner with *ambulare*. Rhætian *na*, beside *anna*, should be identified with Provençal *anar* rather than with Rhætian *amna*, for the reason that a reduction of the group *mmn* to *n* seems to be unparalleled. Rhætian *ala* and *la* are clearly identical with French *aller*; but if we could consult Paris concerning the history of this word, we should be informed once more that although apparently containing the same stem as Provençal *anar*, Spanish *andar*, Portuguese *andar*, Italian *andare*, it has nothing to do with *ambulare*.

Turning to the important group comprising the French, Provençal, Spanish, Portuguese and Italian forms, let us now consider the claims of one of the numerous unpopular etyma, namely *adnare*, "to swim to." This word was first suggested by Muratori in 1739, and has been more or less favored since by Brachet, Canello, Diez, Littré, and Stucke.[2] In the new edition of Körting it heads a list of etyma said to be antiquated by recent investigation. I assume that there existed in later Latin two regular derivatives of *adnare*, namely a frequentative **annitare* and a diminutive **annulare*. Both these forms came into existence after *adnare* had become *annare*. The latter form was felt as a simple verb, for the reason that *nare* had gone out of use. **Annitare* seems to represent a regularization—i.e., an attraction to the regular frequentative type *-itare*—of the attested frequentative *annatare*, rather than a regular new formation from *annare*. It is well known that the endings *-itare* and *-ulare* were living verbal suffixes in later Latin; on this point I refer to Meyer-Lübke, *Rom. Gramm.* II., pp. 611–613. To the examples presenting the termination *-ulare* we may add **brandulare*, "to brandish," from **brandare* (**brandire*), the former giving French *branler*,[3] the latter Provençal *brandar* (Old French *brandir*). The fact that **brandulare* contains a stem of Germanic origin is of obvious chronological significance.

Intervocalic *t* becomes *d* in Spain and Portugal, and may become *d* in Italy. The pretonic vowel of **annitare* > *andare* and that of **vanitare* > *vantare*, "to boast," naturally dropped at different dates; the same phenomenon is attested by Provençal *vandá* < **vannitare*, "to winnow," beside *vantá* < **vanitare*. The Portuguese, Spanish, and Italian development clearly presents no irregularity. Provençal *anar* < *annare* calls for no remark. In French territory we have the series **annulare* > **annlare* > **anlare* > **allare* > *alare* > *aler*, which likewise presents no phonetic irregularity. In Schwan-Behrens' *Altfranzösische Grammatik* (4th ed.), § 186, we are told that French words showing a development of *nl* into

---

[2] Cf. Stucke, pp. 79–88. I find that Stucke, whose book (Darmstadt, 1902) came as this article was undergoing a final revision, suggested the following combination (p. 148): *anar* < *adnare*; *aller* < *adnare* by dissimilation in the phrase *en anar*; *andare* < **ambitare*, a type formed from *ambire*, "to go round," or assumed instead of *ambulare*. It is well known that the formation of **ambitare* from *ambulare* has never been paralleled: **miscitare*, *crepitare*, etc., are from *miscere*, *crepare*, etc.,—not from the corresponding verbs in *-ulare*.

[3] This word has hitherto been explained in various irregular ways.

ndl are not found. The *Dictionnaire général* (I., p. 158, § 484) sets up a sound-law *nl* > *ngl*. The only example given, however, is *espingle*, "pin," said to be from *spinula*, "little thorn." This rather obscure word is derived by Ascoli from **spīcula*, "little pin," and by Paris from **sphingula*, "little sphinx." The variant *espille* may certainly go back to Ascoli's etymon. If *spinula* is the right etymon for *espingle*, the divergence shown by the treatment of *n* + vowel + *l* after the accent, and that of *nn* + vowel + *l* before the accent in proparoxytones, may be attributed to the operation of Neumann's chronological law. An analogical explanation of the form of *espingle* < *spinula* has been suggested by Gröber, *Archiv. f. lat. Lex. u. Gramm.*, V., p. 476; cf. Schwan-Behrens, *l.c.* It should of course be observed, moreover, that the phonetic groups *nl* and *nnl* are not identical.

I now notice in Stucke's treatise (pp. 81–86) a methodical consideration of the vague objections which have been advanced against the semantic development "to swim to," "to go." Stucke finds that the objections will not hold, notes Roumanian *merg*, "to go," from Latin *mergere*, "to plunge" (transitive), and concludes that the shift can by no means be considered impossible. It seems to me that this conclusion is admissible. What fatal objection can be raised, for instance, against the semantic series (1) "to swim to," (2)[4] "to sail to," (3) "to get to," "to go or come to," (4) "to go or come," (5) "to go"? The first step is justified by the existence of Russian *plyt'*, "to swim," "to sail." The passage from (2) to (3) is closely paralleled by the English "to sail into a room," and other similar expressions, in which the proper meaning of the verb "to sail" is often not distinctly felt. The step from (3) to (4), like that from (4) to (5), consists in a simple elimination. We may note in support of (3) and (4) Russian *idtí*, Greek ἔρχομαι, both meaning "to go or come." These parallels certainly show that the series is perfectly legitimate and natural, and, in view of the regularity of the phonetic development, may perhaps seem to make the etymology probable enough. A question of chronological importance, however, should still be considered here. How ancient are the later stages "to sail to," "to get to," "to go or come," "to go"?

Attention has already been called to eighth century glosses like *transgredere* = *ultra alare, transfretavit* = *trans alaret*, which show that at this late date the original meaning had disappeared. Looking about for early evidence, we notice the following passage from Probus, *i.e.* probably Sacerdos, who belongs to the end of the third century (Keil IV., 185, 9):—

---

[4] Professor J. Goebel cites in support of the shorter series "to swim to," "to go to," "to go" the figurative use of German *hereinsegeln, absegeln*—bold expressions for "to come in," "to go off."

Quæritur qua de causa *adno* et non *adnao* dicatur. Hac de causa, quoniam verba primæ coniugationis indicativo modo specie imperfecta ex tertia persona numeri pluralis ultimam syllabam omittunt et *a* sequentem in *o* litteram convertunt et primam personam numeri singularis modi supra dicti ostendunt, ut puta *probabant probo*. Nunc cum dicat Vergilius '*adnabant* pariter' utique iam *adno* non *adnao* facere pronuntiavit.

With this we may compare other queries of the same sort put by this author; *e.g.*, the following:—

182,21: Quæritur qua de causa *calcavi* et non *calcai*[5] dicatur.—182,21: Quæritur qua de causa *coquo* et non *coco* dicatur.—182,28: Quæritur qua de causa Vergilius *fugite* correpte pronuntiarit.—182,38: Quæritur qua de causa *ridere* producto accentu pronuntietur.—185,20: Quæritur qua de causa *fugere* et non *fugire* dicatur.

The form *adnao* and the warning concerning its use recall at once **dao*, **stao*, which were doubtless current in the second and third centuries, and which may be much more ancient. The age of **fao* (> Provençal *fau*) is hard to estimate; but **nao* seems to be a lineal descendant of the prehistoric form **snayo*, on which see Lindsay, *Latin Language*, p. 476. So also probably **stao* < *stáyo* (the prehistoric form of *sto*). The classic forms *no*, *sto* are of later origin, and are modeled after the common type **próbayo* > *probo*. The form **vao* is due to the analogy of *annao*, which it replaced in the Gallic Latin conjugation. Probus' rule clearly shows that *adnare* was a common vulgar word in his time. This, however, at first seems surprising when we remember that the simple verb *nare* had apparently gone out of popular use as early as the classical period. To make the latter point clear, we consult the dictionary (Lewis and Short) and find that *nare*, which is rare even in poets, is cited only twice from prose writers, once from Gellius and once from Columella; and that in the prose passages referred to we have before us an adjectival use of the participle *nans*, "floating" (*nantes scaphae*) and a substantival use of the same participle in the sense of "swimming fowls" (*nantes*). It thus certainly seems that *nare*, which did not survive in Romance, had been replaced before the classical period by the frequentative *natare*, which is quite common in both prose and poetry. Why, then, did *adnare* remain in popular use as late as the third century? It appears that, as early as the first century B. C., the compound must have acquired a meaning approaching that of "to go," which caused it to survive, while *nare* was replaced.

Driven by this striking evidence into a still more ancient period, we consult the *Thesaurus Linguae Latinae*, and now discover that, sure enough,

---

[5] Italian *calcai*, "I trod." The word has also come down into Roumanian, Spanish, Portuguese, Provençal and French. Cf. Körting *s. v. calco*. The ending *ai* for *avi* was the regular vulgar form.

our etymon means in classic Latin not merely "to swim to," "to sail to," but also "to get to." The definition reads thus: "*adnare*, nando accedere ad aliquid; de animantibus; de navibus *et iis quae portant*." The meaning "to swim to" is attested in good prose writers, *e.g.*, in Caesar, *B. C.* 2, 44. The examples presenting the sense "to sail to" are as follows:—

Verg., *Aen.* 1,538: huc pauci vestris adnavimus oris (glossed with the words *adnavigavimus, adnatavimus*); 4,613: Si tangere portus Infandum caput ac terris adnare necesse est.—Ovid., *Trist.* 3, 12, 31: incipient aliquae tamen huc adnare carinae.—Sil. 14, 354: adnabat .... classis subsidio.

The passages certainly seem to show that the acceptation "to sail to" was distinctly poetic in the first century B. C. In the first two passages, the translation "to come to" may seem more accurate; but the context appears to indicate that the notion of "sailing" was clearly present. Forcellini gives a late example of *adnare* used in this sense, which, he says, is equivalent to that of *adnavigare*, from the Auctor *Hist. Datian.*, 13:—

Urbis, quam adnavimus exploratum, materies.

A more important passage is from Cicero, *De Republica* II, 4 (9):—

Sed tamen in his [maritimarum urbium] vitiis inest illa magna commoditas, et quod ubique genitum est [frumentum, merces] ut ad eam urbem, quam incolas, possit *adnare*, et rursus ut id, quod agri efferant sui, quascumque velint in terras portare possint ac mittere.

The explanatory words *frumentum, merces* are added by the editors of the *Thesaurus*. What is the precise force of the word *adnare* as used here? We have, to be sure, a watery context. But can produce swim? Does merchandise sail, and that in precise and sober Latin prose? Turning to Lewis and Short, we are told that *adnare* in this Ciceronian passage means "to come to," "to approach." Perhaps we should not hastily accept the verdict of Latin lexicographers when in doubt as to the meaning of Latin words. As a matter of fact we find that Lewis and Short quote the older reading *gentium* for *genitum*, and seem to be ignorant of the meaning "to sail to." What are we to say, however, of the following?—

Cicero, *Tusc.* 4, 14, 33: Habes ea quæ de perturbationibus enucleate disputant Stoici quæ λογικά appellant, quia disseruntur subtilius. Ex quibus quoniam tanquam e scrupulosis cotibus *enavigavit oratio*, reliquæ disputationis cursum teneamus.— *Tusc.* 5, 30, 87: Eadem Calliphontis erit Diodirique sententia, quoniam uterque honestatem sic complectitur, ut omnia, quæ sine ea sint, longe retro ponenda censeat. Reliqui habere se angustius videntur; *enatant* tamen.—*Imp. Pomp.* 12, 24: Quis enim umquam aut obeundi negotii aut consequendi quæstus studio tam brevi tempore tot loca adire, tantos cursus conficere potuit, quam celeriter Cn. Pompeio duce *belli impetus navigavit?*—Petronius *Satir.* 57, 29 (ed. Bücheler, 1882): Habebam *in domo* qui mihi pedem opponerent hac illac; tamen—*enatavi.*—Florus 2, 2, 17: Regulo duce, iam in Africam *navigabat bellum.*—2, 8, 1: Madedoniam Asia statim et regem Philippum Antiochus excepti quodam casu, quasi de industria sic adgubernante fortuna, ut quem ad modum ab Africa in Achaiam, sic ab Achaia in Asiam ultro se suggerentibus causis imperium procederet, et cum terrarum orbis situ ipse *ordo victoriarum navigaret.*—Sil. III, 662: *Has* observatis *valles enavimus* astris.

Lewis and Short say that *enare* in the last passage means "to sail through." If this is right, the sailing is evidently figurative. The force of Latin poetic figures is often hard to estimate, and the passage, which was noted by Brachet, may not by itself establish much. The significance of the quotations in prose, however, two of which have already been cited by Cornu in support of the etymon *enatare*, is unmistakable. It has already been noticed by lexicographers, and is certainly obvious, that philosophers do not swim out of arguments, that a Ciceronian discussion does not sail out of difficulties, and that a war movement does not sail. The passages clearly establish for the classical period a time-worn metaphor, which had been handed down by oral tradition in the words *enatare, enavigare*, "to get out" and *navigare*, "to go or come," as well as in *adnatare* and *adnare*, "to get to." After all, we have no reason to be surprised at the venerable look of the figure. The chronology of *nare* alone indicates that we must assign to some prehistoric age the very stage of our series which, at first blush, we might assume to be almost modern, namely the figurative sense "to go or come to." Indeed we now recall Greek νέομαι, "to go," beside νέω, "to swim," *"to sail," which might lead one to assign this stage to a Graeco-Italic period. But words of similar meaning should never be hastily identified if the phonetic connection seems obscure. In this very instance, the existence of νίσσομαι, "to go," raises a doubt regarding the prehistoric form of νέομαι, making the connection of the latter word with νέω appear dubious. At any rate, we have located the origin of the Romance sense in a prehistoric Latin age. We may now indicate how and why the changes in meaning occurred.

In some remote prehistoric period, certainly many thousand years ago, something like a ship was invented. The invention was called apparently a "swimmer" (ναῦς, *navis*), for the reason that it was said to "swim," *i.e.*, to sail (νέϝω, *nare*). On this connection, see Vaniček, *Etymologisches Wörterbuch*, pp. 1158 ff. For thousands of years *nare* was a common word meaning both "to swim" and "to sail." In fact, we find it still used in both senses, not to mention that of "to fly," by poets of the classical period. At this date, however, it had grown rare and bookish. It had been replaced in the speech of the people by the Ciceronian frequentative *natare*, "to swim," and the secondary formation *nav-ig-are*, "to sail." The words for "to sail" readily assume figurative senses in all languages, and prehistoric Latin was not an exception to the rule. Hundreds of years before the opening of the Christian era, *nare* began to be used to describe the motion of persons on land. At first the usage was felt as a figure of speech, like the humorous English "to navigate," and later as a bold expression, like the English "to sail down the street."

The compound *enare* was used in the same way, with the same picturesque connotation, whence later both *enavigare* and *enatare*, "to get out"; and likewise *adnare*, whence later *adnatare* and doubtless *adnavigare*, "to get to." In the course of centuries the compounds *adnare*, *adnatare* became more and more common in the new figurative sense, and more and more rare in the earlier meanings. The picturesque connotation grew fainter and fainter in proportion, until finally it was lost and forgotten. To the uneducated Roman of Caesar's day, *adnare* meant scarcely more than "to get to": his words for "to swim to," "to sail to" were *adnatare*, *adnavigare* and *natare ad*, *navigare ad*. Prose writers of the classical period doubtless tried to avoid the improper sense of *adnare* in dignified composition, although they had no objection to the somewhat antiquated meaning "to swim to"; while poets admitted the archaic sense "to sail to." The fact that *adnatare*, *"to get to," is not attested in familiar passages, as is *enatare*, "to get out," is purely accidental. After the phonetic development of *adnare* into *annare*, which doubtless belongs to an early post-classical period, the compound nature of the word was no longer recognizable, and the meaning "to go or come to" naturally became "to go or come"—a stage attested by Papias' well-known gloss: *adnare*, *adnatare* = *venire*. The primary meaning of *adnatare* was felt for some time after that of *adnare* was forgotten, for the reason that *natare* (beside **notare*), "to swim," remained in vulgar use. In later Latin, however, *annatare*, "to swim to" was completely replaced by *natare ad*, and this replacement brought about the loss of the connotation in *annatare*, "to go or come (to)," after which the regularized form **annitare* beside **annulare* (< *annare*) came into use. Schuchardt (*Rom.* XVII., p. 418) has pointed out that the boundary line between the territories of the verbs "to go" and "to come" is vague: *allons, allez, andiamo, andate* may still often be translated as "come!" *Aller* may have had the meaning "to come" oftener in Old French than it has at present; cf. Froissart, Bartsch-Horning *Chrestomathie* (7th ed.), col. 434, ll. 31 ff.:—

> Adont lui ala il souvenir de Phelippe d'Artevelle, e dist a ceulx qui entour lui estoient, "Ce Phelippe, si il est ou vif ou mort, je le verroie moult voulontiers."

The almost complete exclusion of the notion "to come" may be attributed to the influence of *vado, vadis, vadit, vade, vadunt*, from *vadere*, "to go," which replaced the corresponding forms of *adnare* in the Romance conjugation.

The principal new points brought out in this paper may be summed up as follows. In the first place, we have called attention to the fact that the derivation of the Romance group from *adnare*, "to swim to" presents no phonetic irregularity. We have set up a simple semantic series, which is proved by parallels to be legitimate and natural. Reference to the Latin dictionary has shown that the assumed sense-development is not even hypothetical. We have found the stages "to sail to," "to go or come to," attested in classic Latin, and the latter use confirmed by the analogous sense of *enatare, enavigare, navigare, enare*. We have called attention to the replacement of *nare* by *natare* and *navigare*, and of *adnatare*, "to swim to," by *natare ad*, which caused the primary meanings of *adnare* and *adnatare* to fall gradually into oblivion. We have proved by a quotation from Probus that *adnare* actually remained vulgar in later Latin. We have pointed out that after the phonetic development of *adn* into *ann*, *adnare, adnatare*, "to go or come to" would naturally have meant "to go or come." Indeed we find even this stage attested in Latin. In short, we have not only shown that the assumed changes in meaning did occur, but have also been able to indicate when, how, and why they occurred. Perhaps the derivation of *anar, andare, andar, aller*, "to go," from Latin *annare*, *annitare*, *annulare*, "to go or come," will now seem plausible.[6]

[6] Table of derivations:—

Roumanian *imbla* / Roumanian *umbla*	"to walk,"		*ambulare*, "to walk."
Roumanian *merg*			*mergere*, "to plunge" (trans.).
Western Roumanian *ëmna* / Macedo-Roumanian *imnare* / Istrian *amna* / Rhætian *amna*		*amminare*, < *"to go"	*adminare*, "to chase to," "to drive to."
Rhætian *ma*			*meare*, "to go."
French *aller* / Rhætian *ala, la*	*annulare*, "to go or come"	< *annare*, "to go or come"	< *adnare*, "to get to," "to sail to," "to swim to."
Rhætian *anna, na* / Provençal *anar*		*annare*, "to go or come"	< *adnare*, "to get to," "to sail to," "to swim to."
Italian *andare*	*annitare*, "to go or come"	< *annatare*, "to go or come"	< *adnatare*, *"to get to," "to swim to" (cf. *enatare*, "to get out," "to swim out")
Spanish *andar*			< *adnare*, "to get to," "to sail to," "to swim to."
Portuguese *andar*		< *annare*, "to go or come"	< *adnare*, "to get to," "to sail to," "to swim to."

IV

ITALIAN *ANDARE; AGIO; MALVAGIO*

1. It. *Andare*, Prov. *Annar*, F. *Aller*: A Rejoinder

Revewers hav not accuratly appraisd my *Etimology ov the Romance Words for To Go*.[1] Inasmuch as the article appeard in 1904 and contributions to the subject seem rather scarce nowadays, I propose to take up the subject again.

I will express no opinion ov Horning's essay.[2] He merely refers to a detail ov my article in a foot-note. Elise Richter[3] has lately written ov "the solution ov the *andare* problem, which Horning sturdily attacks and which he has eminently advanst." Just how, she does not say. But we used to hear ov *la question ambulare*, point-blank; so somhow a little ground is being gaind, whoever gets the credit. Schuchardt[4] seems to abandon his monogenetic scheme by admitting that his tipe **ambitare* may be connected with *ambire* rather than with *ambulare*. Behrens,[5] referring to my work, uses the frase "noteworthy but hardly convincing." From this authority I shud hav expected a detaild and definit appreciation at least ov the French morfology and fonology involvd in my hipothesis. P. Meyer[6] says that from the postulated Vulgar Latin verbs **annitare* and **annulare* 'by various slight-ov-hand tricks we get to the Spanish and French verbs—all this not very serious.' Any fonologist who reads my article will admit that this is hardly a justified presentation.

I will consider in detail the report or rather discussion ov my article by Elise Richter.[7] Fräulein Richter fails to notis my derivations ov dialectic Roumanian *amna, imna* from **adminare*, "to chase to," and ov F. *branler* from **brandulare*. A much more serious neglect, to my mind, is the utter ignoring ov my carefully, fully, clearly and painstakingly elaborated scheme ov the Latin-Romance sense-development ov *adnare, annare, *annitare, *annulare*; *viz.* 1) "to swim to," 2) "to sail to" (well attested),

---

[1] *Publications ov the Modern Language Association ov America*, New Series, xii, 217 ff.

[2] *Zeitschrift f. rom. Phil.*, xxix (1905), p. 515.

[3] *Jahresbericht über die Fortschritte der romanischen Philologie*, ix (1905, printed 1909), i, 67.

[4] *Z. f. rom. Phil.*, xxx (1906), p. 84.

[5] *Z. f. rom. Phil.*, xxxi (1907), p. 123.

[6] *Romania*, xxxvi (1907), p. 140.

[7] *Jahresbericht ü. d. Fort. d. rom. Phil.*, viii (1904, printed 1906–08), i, 85 f.

3) "to get to," "to go or com to" (once attested as a meaning ov *adnare* in classic Latin, cf. *enatare*, "to get out" [in Cicero]), 4) "to go or com" (cf. Russian *idti*, Greek ἔρχεσθαι[8] with both meanings, and note Papias' gloss *adnare adnatare venire*), 5) "to go" (occasionally rather "to com"). As I might have expected from the *Jahresbericht* critic, however, I find here somthing like a just appreciation ov the fonological and morfological matters involvd in the derivations *aller* < *annulare, *andare* < *annitare. My critic, be it noted, reluctantly accepts the important and tell-tale derivation *annar* < *annare*, mentioning as evidential the monition *non adnao sed adno*, which I discoverd in the grammarian Probus. She does not attack the fonology ov the French derivation. Her definit[9] objections ar confined to two points in morfology which ar well delt with in my former article but which I will now discuss again, namely the use ov the suffixes *-itare* and *-ulare* in Vulgar Latin. On the first I hav only to quote Meyer-Lübke's list,[10] including *circitare, *cogitare*, *flavitare, *miscitare, *movitare, *nasitare, *pigritare, *seditare, *sequitare, *taxitare, *tinnitare*, *vanitare, *vannitare, *visitare*. As tho unaware ov this array, my critic ventures to assert in the *Annual Report on the Progress ov Romance Filology*, "In Spanish *andar* < *adnare*, with the metathesis ov *dn* > *nd*, common in Spanish, wud be more acceptable than derivation from *annitare." Does not this reactionary suggestion also betray ignorance ov the antiquity ov the reduction ov *dn* to *nn* in Latin?—On the suffix *-ulare* I hav alredy refered Meyer-Lükke.[11] I now mention the postulated or reconstructed Vulgar Latin diminutiv verbs which survived in the vernacular ov northern Gaul, viz., *brustulare > *brûler*, *misculare > *mêler*, *orulare > *ourler*,[12] *rasiculare[13] > *racler*, *turbulare > *troubler*. To this group I hav added *brandulare > *branler* and *annulare > *aller*. It is held that new formations in *-ulare* wud rather be expected in Italian than in French. This objection was foreseen and carefully met in my article. The etima *annulare, *brandulare wer postulated in the Vulgar Latin period along with the other postulata just cited. I translate a few interesting but to me unconvincing comments from the *Jahresbericht* article:

"The formation ov a diminutiv ov a verb for "to go" seems somwhat strange anyway. It cud scarcely originate in the nursery. It wud, perhaps, be used to a dog. [*Footnote*: Cf. Viennese *ausserl* = "get out," dim.

---

[8] This word was suggested by Mr. E. W. Martin of Stanford University.
[9] I quote her indefinit objections later on.
[10] *Rom. Gram.*, II, § 587.
[11] *Rom. Gram.*, II, p. 611.
[12] This verb is properly from *ourle* < *orula.
[13] This diminutiv ov *rasicare, the well establisht modification ov classic *radere*, was constructed by Diez and mistakenly rejected by Körting.

ov *aussi*, said to the dog.] The main objection, as in the case ov all other hipotheses, remains, that these formations, ov greater or lesser fonetic accuracy, ar vain suppositions, while the existence ov *ambulare* is establisht, whether its fonetic development is explicable or not."

I quite agree that, to quote my critic's expression, "die Existenz von *ambulare* feststeht." I fail to see any enormous difficulty, however, in explaining the fonetic development ov the Latin verb for German *gehen*, which became Roumanian *imbla*, French *ambler*, English *amble*. Filologists will recognize Fräulein Richter's avowd preference for Bovet's application ov the Wulff suggestion (see her article) as temporizing and unprogressiv rather than pacific. She here follows Paris, who, however in seeming to grant som grace to the delta or thick *l* notion, apparently used this device to mark with a warning (Δ) the approach to other hopeless but more pretentious *ambulare* alleys.

2. It. *Agio, agiato*, Port. *Azo*, Prov. *Aize*, F. *Aise, Aisé*, etc.

I. The Forms. Verbs: It. *adagiare, agiare*, Prov. *aisar, aizir, aisir*, O. F. *aasier, aisier* (with opposit meaning, *malaisier*), *aiser*. Nouns: It. *agio (malagio)*, Prov. *ais, aize, aise, aisimens*, Cat. *aise*, Port. *azo*, F. *aise (malaise), aisance*, Eng. *ease*. Adjectivs: It. *agiato* (earlier also *malagiato*), F. *aise, aisé (malaisé)*, Eng. *easy*.

II. Controversy. The derivation from Latin *ansa*, proposed by Bugge, is refuted by Thomas, *Mélanges d'étymologie française*, p. 22, who particularly insists that in vew ov the "constant" spelling ov the Provençal words, in the best sources, with a *z*, an etimon in *sy* is impossible. Mackel assumes the existence ov a Vulgar Latin **adatiare* < Germanic **asatia* supported by Gothic "azēti, st. n., Annehmlichkeit" (Körting's summary). Here the assumed shift from Germanic *s* to Vulgar Latin *d* is quite strange. Thomas (*op. cit.*, p. 223), arguing against Mackel's etimology, asserts that in Prov., **atiare* cud hav becom only **azar*, which wud not account for a verbal substantiv *aize*. This, however, is not so; witness *potionem* > *pozon, poizon, rationem* > *razo, raizon*, etc.[14] It is plain that a tipe **atiare* cud hav becom **aizar* in Prov. The derivation by Thomas (following in part Darmesteter) from *adjacens, adjacentia*, fights shy ov the Port. and It. forms,—a neglect which may be said to invalidate the suggested etimology.

III. Contribution. Mackel's tipe **adatiare* is substantially not incorrect, a V. L. word in *ty* being postulated by the developments. I posit the form **malatiare* (cf. It. *malato* < **malatus*), whence, by a change ov the (mistaken) prefix, **adatiare*, "to make good," "to make easy," and by aferesis ov the mistaken initial sillable **atiare*. Note the regularity ov the

[14] Cf. Grandgent, *Provençal Phonology, and Morphology*, p. 68.

assumed developments *malatiatus > F. malaisé, It. malagiato, *malatiare > O. F. malaisier. Port. azo (postverbal) is regular.[15] Meyer-Lübke[16] states, "IARE tritt an Participia und Adjectiva, gehört aber naturgemäss der vorromanischen Zeit an." He presents dozens ov examples. The process ov postverbal or deverbal derivation ov nouns and adjectivs is also well establisht.[17] Meyer-Lübke[18] indicates by a score ov examples and several etceteras the commonness ov the prefix mal. Considering the numerous pairs like contentus beside *malcontentus, with opposit meanings, I suppose that the form *malatiatus was taken for a compound, the second hâf ov which was *atiatus, with meaning opposit to that ov *malatiatus. A similar confusion is attested by O. F. empouiller beside dépouiller < despoliare. Cf. also It. bonaccia, "câm" for *malaccia < malacia.

3. It. Malvagio, O. S. Malvazo, Sp., Port. Malvado, Prov. Malvatz, F. Mauvais.

It seems unnecessary to show that the various theories hitherto proposed to account for the origin ov these words ar all unsatisfactory. Diez, starting from O. S. malvar, "böse machen," derives it from male levare, an etimon ov suitable meaning presenting no fonetic irregularity; but he separates malvado and malvagio, which seem related. I suggest the assumption ov a V. L. verb derived from male levatus > Sp. malvado, Prov. malvatz—viz., *mal(e) levatiare > It. *malvagiare, O. F. malvaisier, O. S. *malvazar, Prov. *malvaizar. The surviving It. malvagio, F. mauvais, together with O. S. malvazo, Prov. malvais ar postverbals. On post-verbals in general see Meyer-Lübke.[19] The fonetic changes assumed ar all regular. (Prov. malvaitz is a contamination ov malvatz and malvais.)

[15] Cf. Gröber's Grundriss, I, p. 748.
[16] Rom. Gram., II, p. 606.
[17] Cf. Meyer-Lübke, Rom. Gram., II, pp. 441–448.
[18] Rom. Gram. II, p. 570.
[19] Rom. Gram., II, pp. 376, 448.

V

ANAR-ANDARE-ALLER < -ADNARE-*ANNITARE-*ANNULARE

In 1905 I publisht in *PMLA*[1] a monogenetic derivation of Provençal *anar*, Italian *andare*, Spanish and Portuguese *andar*, French *aller* 'to go' from Latin *adnare* 'to swim to,' 'to sail to', *'to get to'. Shortly after its appearance my article was reviewed by Elisa Richter[2], whose objections I met in a second article[3]. Richter accepted the derivation of *anar* from *adnare*, but questioned the etyma *annitare and *annulare because they are unattested and seemed surprising. Körting[4] thought the etymology *anar-andare-aller* < *annare-*annitare-*annulare* both phonetically and semantically acceptable; but Meyer-Lübke failed to mention it in the last two editions of his dictionary[5], and as my complete solution of this old problem has therefore sometimes been overlookt by competent scholars in recent years, I now present a brief restatement of its leading features.

The postulation of Vulgar Latin *annitare is quite simple, such formations being common. The diminutive *annulare has a recognized suffix attested by less numerous examples. The morphological series *annare-*annitare-*annulare is paralleled exactly by the series *miscere-*miscitare-*misculare > Spanish *mecer*, Italian *mestare*, French *mêler* (Spanish *mezclar*). Richter's remark that *annulare "could hardly have originated in the nursery" is inconsequential; for inasmuch as the etymology *mêler* < *misculare is accepted without explanation of the cause of the substitution of the simple by the suffixt verb, the formation of *annulare, a diminutive of *annare, must be regarded as morphologically correct and likely, whether it was originally used in reference to children or not.

The obviously regular phonetic development of Provençal *anar* < *annare* < *adnare* supplies the key to the whole mystery: with the stem *ann-* and the suffixes *-itare*, *-ulare*, the modern verbs *andare*, *andar*, and *aller* may be seen to have developt regularly, in spite of the common assumption that their development must have contravened phonetic law. The syncope of *annitare is certainly regular in Hispanic, as in *vindicare* > *vengar*, etc.; and notwithstanding the absence of parallel examples of *nn-t*, it may reasonably be asserted, in view of the close analogy of *carricare* > Spanish and Old Portuguese *cargar*, *caballicare* > Sp. *cabalgar*,

[1] 19.217–233.
[2] *Jahresbericht über die Fortschritte der romanischen Philologie* 8.85 ff (1904).
[3] *PMLA* 26.333–336 (1911).
[4] *Lateinisch-romanisches Wörterbuch*, 3rd ed.
[5] *Romanisches etymologisches Wörterbuch*.

Previously unpublished.

Port. *cavalgar*, that Spanish and Portuguese *andar* is the regular phonetic reflex of **annitare*. The case is similar in Tuscan: while other words containing the group *nn-t* are wanting, the analogy of Veronese and Savoyan *vandá* < **vannitare* 'to flail'[6] indicates that the *t* in **annitare* became *d* in accordance with phonetic law. The regularity of the phonetic development **annulare* > French *aller* (Old French *aler*) is, in view of the phonetic elements involved, prima facie highly probable, and therefore, in the absence of other words containing the group *nn-l*, Gamillscheg's misleading statement[7] that the derivation of *aller* from **annulare* is phonetically impossible may safely be set down as the baseless assertion of an advocate of the phonetically unfit etymon *ambulare*, which became French *ambler* (English *amble*), and can only be connected with *aller* by quite objectionable phonetic procedure. Another blunder in Gamillscheg's entry on *aller* may be noticed in the asterisk which he writes before the attested Latin word *adnare*. He uses another asterisk to indicate, in conformity with his system of signs, that he has not seen my first article in *PMLA*[7a], to which he refers, and which he essays to controvert in the manner mentioned.

The etymology *anar-andare-aller* < *adnare-*annitare-*annulare* should therefore be recognized as correct. It explains all the pertinent linguistic facts without *ad hoc* assumptions, and without separating the French, Hispanic, and Italian words for "to go", which most scholars have always regarded as genetically related.[8] It rests solidly on its simple phonology, involving no known irregularities, on the clear morphological parallel *miscere-*miscitare-*misculare* > *mecer-mestare-mêler*, and on the reasonable postulation of the ancient semantic shift 'swim to' > 'sail to' (attested) > *'get to', this unattested sense being demonstrated by the attested colloquial meaning of *enatare* 'swim out'—'get out'. That *enatare* did have the colloquial meaning 'to get out' is proved by the following passages: Cicero, *Tusculanae Disputationes* 5, 30, 87: Eadem Calliphontis erit Diodorique sententia, quoniam uterque honestatem sic complectitur, ut omnia, quae sine ea sint, longe retro ponenda censeat. Reliqui habere angustius videntur; ENATANT tamen.—Petronius, *Satirae* 57, 29 (ed. Bücheler, 1882): Habebam in domo qui mihi pedem opponerent hac illac; tamen—ENATAVI.

[6] Recorded by Meyer-Lübke, *REW*[3], s.v. **vannitare*.

[7] *Etymologisches Wörterbuch der französischen Sprache* (1928).

[7a] Pp. 12–22 above.

[8] Recent etymologies of *aller* which must be declared improbable because they separate *aller* from *anar* and *andare* as well as for other reasons, but which at any rate prove that the derivation of *aller* from *ambulare* is not accepted by all Romance scholars of the present day, are as follows: *aller* < **allare—allatus* (E. F. Parker, *PMLA* 49.1025–1031 [1934]); *aller* < *ad-de-illa(c)* + *are* (J. D. M. Ford, in the volume of studies dedicated to José Leite de Vasconcellos and publisht in Portugal [according to W. F. Manning, *Language* 13.186f.]); *aller* < **ad-iterare* (W. F. Manning, *Language* 13.186–193 [1937]).

VI

FRENCH *FLÉCHIR*, SPANISH *ROSCA*, *SESGO;* FRENCH *RUCHE*

French *fléchir* < Old French *fleschir* < *fleschier,* "to bend," < **flexicāre* < *flexus* < *flectere,* "to bend."
French *fléchir*, O. F. *fleschir, fleskir* has been derived by Förster, *Zeitschrift f. rom. Phil.,* III, p. 262, from a Latin **fleskire* < **flescus* < *flexus.* The assumption of the shift of *ks* and *sk* is defended by an appeal to *alaskir* from *laxus*, seemingly showing the same metathesis. This phonetic step, which must be assigned to a Latin period, is in both instances certainly unjustifiable, although it has been admitted by excellent authorities. In the *Dictionnaire général* we find French *lâcher* derived from a type **lascare* < *laxare.* Here the assumption of metathesis seems to go back to Diez, *Etymologisches Wb.,* pp. 188 f., who cites as analoga Campanian *fisquer* for *fixer* and *lusque* for *luxe;* but these forms clearly represent popular deformations of learned words and are accordingly irrelevant. French *lâcher* has also been derived by Gröber, who evidently objects to the dubious metathesis, from Old High German **lasc,* a type assumed to account for Middle High German *lasch,* "schlaff," and Old Norse *lǫskr,* "schlaff," "lass." Kluge, however (*Etymologisches Wb.,* 6th ed.), is inclined to derive the Germanic from the Romance group. Gröber's derivation has also been disputed on phonological grounds by Mackel; cf. Körting, s. v. **lask,* who rejects the Germanic etymon. The correct etymon for *lâcher,* namely **laxicare,* was first suggested by Ulrich, *Zeitschrift. f. rom. Phil.,* IX, p. 429; is rejected by Körting, who says that the assumption of the type is unnecessary and seems to consider the derivation of the French word unsettled; but is accepted by Meyer-Lübke, *Rom. Gramm.,* II, p. 608. It will be seen later that **laxicare* presents a perfect phonetic type for the derivation of the French form. The cognate Romance forms (Provençal *lascar,* etc.) present no difficulty. Returning to *fléchir,* we need only mention the derivation of the word from *flectere,* adopted by Diez, which is phonetically impossible. Paris, *Rom.,* VIII, p. 628, has explained *fléchir* as derived from the adjective *flesche,* "bent," and the latter as a postverbal from *fleschier,* which he derives from **flescare* for *flexare.* My objections to this etymology are as follows. In the first place, the existence of the adjective *flesche* is extremely doubtful. Scheler and Paris (*l. c.*) thought it occurred in one Old French passage, namely, in the *Saint Eloi,* 92 b: *Genous fleches, enclin le chief.* Here Förster, however (article cited), reads flechés, and the passage is also quoted in this form by Godefroy. No evidence for the

existence of the word has appeared in Godefroy's *Complément*, and under the circumstances it should doubtless be regarded as imaginary. In the second place, the phonetic step from *flexare* to **flescare* is without support. Finally Gröber, *Archiv. f. lat. Lex. u. Gr.*, II, p. 285, explains *fléchir* as a collateral form of *flechier* showing a change of conjugation. This explanation certainly seems to be the correct one. A glance at the lexicon is sufficient to convince one that verbs fluctuating between the *-ir* and *-(i)er* conjugations were fairly common in Old French: note, *e. g.*, *refroidier*, *refroidir*; *embalsemer*, *embalsamir*; *engrossier*, *engrossir*; *amplier*, *amplir*; *empoenter*, *empoentir*; *empreignier*, *empreignir*. The list could undoubtedly be greatly lengthened.

Now, to explain this earlier form *flechier*, Gröber (article cited) sets up a type **flecticare*, which is accepted by Körting, but which does not account for the Old French form *fleschier*. Paris and Förster (articles cited) assume that the regular Old French form of both *flechier* and *flechir* had an *s*, and, in view of the spellings with *s* cited by Förster, this opinion certainly seems to be correct. Several forms with *s* will also be seen in Godefroy.

The right etymon is **flexicare*. This type was first suggested by Gröber (article cited), who rejected it on the ground that it should have given O. F. **fleischier*. For a similar reason the *Dictionnaire général* rejects **taxitare* as the etymon of O. F. *taster*, Modern French *tâter*, alleging that this Latin type would have given O. F. **taister*. But both authorities are in error regarding the sound-law here in question, which is stated by Schwan-Behrens, *Altfranz. Gramm.*, 4th ed., § 158, 2, as follows:—

"Völlige Assimilation des Palatals an den folgenden Konsonanten trat .... in vortoniger Stellung in der Verbindung ks + Kons. ein: Beispiele: .... *sextariu* > *sestier*, *dextrariu* > *destrier*, **tax(i)tare* > *taster*, *entox(i)care* > *entoschier*, *extendere* > *estendre*, *extorquere* > *estordre*, satzunbetonte *extra* > *estre* und *joxta* > *juste*."

To these examples we may now add **flexicare* > *fleschier*, which is perfectly analogous to *intoxicare* > *entoschier*, **laxicare* > *laschier*, and **taxicare* > *taschier*. *Tâcher*, the modern form of *taschier*, is derived by the *Dictionnaire général* from **tascare*, a metathesized form of *taxare*. But, as has been shown above, the analoga seemingly justifying the assumption of a metathesis of the group *ks* in a Latin period are of no value. The etymon **taxicare* is due to Ulrich, *Zeitschrift f. rom. Phil.*, IX, p. 429. It is put in brackets by Körting, but is accepted by Meyer-Lübke, *Rom. Gramm.*, II, p. 608.[1] The fact that a so-called epenthetic *i* dies not appear in developments like that of **taxitare* > *taster* is to be explained by the

---

[1] The daring etymology *tâche* < **tasca* < **τάσχις* < *τάξις*, recently suggested by T. Claussen, *Romanische Forschungen*, XV (1904), p. 847, scarcely deserves mention. The *Dictionnaire général* correctly states that *tâche* is a postverbal from *tâcher*.

chronology of the sound-change. It is well known that the pretonic vowel in paroxytones and the posttonic vowel in proparoxytones dropped at different dates. Thus *taxitare, as is evidently assumed by Schwan-Behrens, *l. c.* had been reduced to *tastare in a period when *taxitat was still trisyllabic. One might of course also expect a form of the verb with epenthetic *i*, preserved from the proparoxytone forms, to survive, and this actually did happen in some cases. We need only cite the postverbal *test* beside *tast*, presupposing a form *taister beside *taster*, and the still more striking form *entoischier* beside *entoschier* < *intoxicare*.

If this reasoning is correct, we have established a conclusion diametrically opposed to that of the *Dictionnaire général*, s. v. *fléchir*, which says with regard to the etymology of the word: ' Origine inconnue. La forme du mot ne permet pas d'y voir un représentant, direct ou indirect, du latin *flectere*, qui a cependant le même sens."

Spanish *rosca*, "screw" < *rōsicare < *rōsus* < *rōdere*, "to gnaw."

In Monlau's *Diccionario etymológico* we find the following note: "Rosca: 'Es del vascuence *errosca*, y se dijo de *erruzca*, á fuerza, por la grande que tiene para mover grandes pesos.' (Larramendi.) Según Covarrubias viene del latín *ruere*, lanzarse, arrojarse, porque gira sobre sí misma. Diez afirma, con más acierto, que el orígen de *rosca* es todavía desconocido." The word is missing in Körting's index. On consulting the recent edition of the dictionary of the Spanish Academy, we are told that *rosca* is derived from an absurd Greek etymon.

I derive the word from *rosicare, "to gnaw," the existence of which in late Latin is rendered certain by Italian *rosicare*, Provençal *rosegar*, "to gnaw." The etymology presents no phonetic irregularity. For the *c*, cf. *rascar*, "to scratch" < *rasicare, "to scratch." There is no reason for doubting that intervocalic *c* in this position, in Spanish as in Provençal and French, may either remain a surd or become a sonant, according to the date at which the preceding vowel dropped. The formation of *rosca*, "a gnawing instrument" as a postverbal from *rosicare, "to gnaw," has countless parallels, for which I refer to Meyer-Lübke, *Rom. Gramm.*, II, pp. 444 ff. I need only mention Italian *leva*, "lever," from *levare*, "to raise." For the sense-development we may compare English *bit, i.e.*, apparently "a biting instrument," and Italian *succhiare*, "to bore," generally derived from *sucular, "to suck." *Rosicare may have a direct descendant in the Spanish technical word *roscar*, "to furrow," which, however, may also be a recent derivative from *rosca*.

Spanish *sesgo*, "oblique" < *sesgar*, "to cut obliquely" < *sēsecāre, "to cut apart."

To explain Spanish *sesgo*, "oblique," Baist, *Zeitschrift f. rom. Phil.*, VII, p. 122, sets up a type **sēsecus*, which he attempts to support by the analogy of *circumsecus, extrinsecus*. The formation of **sēsecus* is not made sufficiently probable, and the etymon is rightly rejected by Körting, who favors the derivation from **subsecare*. The latter type, however, presents insuperable phonetic difficulty, to say nothing of semantic obscurity. Ulrich, *Zeitschrift für rom. Phil.*, IV, p. 383, derived *sesgar* from **sĕxicare* < **sexus* < *sectus*, but Körting objects to the etymology on the ground that **sexus* for *sectus* is a monstrosity. **Sĕxicare* also presents phonetic and semantic difficulty.

The right etymon is **sēsecāre*, "to cut apart," an unimpeachable formation presenting no phonetic irregularity. This type was also thought of by Baist (article cited), who dismissed it on account of the existence of the adjective *sesgo*. But the derivation of *sesgo* as a postverbal from *sesgar* presents no difficulty. On the formation of postverbal adjectives I refer to Meyer-Lübke, *Rom. Gramm.*, II, p. 448, and to the *Dictionnaire général*, I, § 53. The sense-development also presents no difficulty: 1) "to cut apart," "to cut across;" 2) "cut across," "oblique."

French *ruche*, "hive" (beside *rouche*, "hull of a ship on the stocks") < O. F. *rusche*, Prov. *rusca*, Piedmontese and Lombard *rusca*, "bark," < Comascan *ruscá*, "to scale off," < **rŭspicare* < **ruspare*, "to scratch." In the *Dictionnaire général* we are told that *ruche* is of Celtic origin. Körting's article on the word reads as follows:—

"*Rūsca* ist das vorauszusetzende, aber bezüglich seines Ursprunges ganz dunkle Grundwort zu prov. *rusca*, Baumrinde (auch piemont. und lomb. *rusca*); altfrz. *rusche* (norm. *ruque*), neufrz. *ruche* (aus Baumrinde gefertigter Bienenkorb, Schiffsrumpf). Diez 673 hielt das Wort für keltisch, Thurneysen, p. 111, verneint dies."

To make it clear that the words for "hive" and "bark" are identical, Diez, *l. c.*, cites Spanish *corcho*, meaning both "bark of the cork-tree" and "bee-hive." I propose to derive the group from the verbal type **rŭspicare*, which seems to explain perfectly all the forms. For the dropping of the middle vowel in Provençal and French we may compare Latin *hospitale* > Prov. *ostal*, O. F. *ostel*. In Tuscan, *hospitale* becomes *ospedale*, retaining the pretonic vowel. But Meyer-Lübke, *Italienische Grammatik*, p. 71, notes that the Italian dialects diverge widely from Florentine in their treatment of syncope, and in view of the vagueness of our present knowledge of the whole question I hold that, unless the contrary assumption can be supported by evidence, we should admit the regularity of the development of **ruspicare* into an early Italian **ruscare*, surviving in Comascan as *ruscá*, whence as postverbals Piedmontese and Lombard *rusca*. We may perhaps cite Tuscan *tastare* < **taxitare*, *destare* < **de-excitare* as showing a development parallel to that assumed, though, to be sure, the consonant-groups in question are quite different. This verb **ruspicare* is derived readily enough, by the elimination of the common suffix *-icare*, from **ruspare*, the existence of which in Latin with the original meaning of "to scratch" is generally admitted by Romance scholars, *e. g.*, by Diez, Körting, and Schuchardt (*Romanische Etymologieen*, I, p. 27) on account of the existence of Latin *ruspari*, "to examine," and Italian *ruspare*, "to scratch." The semantic series,—1) "to scratch off," "to peel," 2) "peel," "bark," 3) "hive made of bark," 4) "hive,"—seems perfectly legitimate, particularly in view of the fact that the first stage is supported by Comascan *ruscá*, "to scale off."

VII

SPANISH *ESTRAGAR; SESGAR; SIMADO; SOSEGAR*

1. *Estragar* 'to spoil', *estrago* 'ravage'.

It is plain that the noun is not derived from the Latin noun *strages*, but is a postverbal formation. Meyer-Lübke, in his *Romanisches etymologisches Wörterbuch*, postulates a Vulgar Latin **stragicare*, 'verheeren', evidently connecting this type with *strages*, as **caballicare* is formed from *caballus*. However, it is questionable whether **stragicare* would have developt into Spanish *estragar*. An analogous word, *cogitare*, becomes *cuidar* in Spanish. Meyer-Lübke, *Romanische Grammatik* 1. 444, indicates the regularity of the development *cogito* > *cuido*; likewise R. Menéndez Pidal, *Manual elemental de gramática española*[3] 66,110. Since no clear case of the development of Latin *-agicare* into Spanish *-agar* has ever been cited, it seems reasonable to hold that the type **stragicare* would have developt into **estraigar* in Spanish.

I postulate the type **stragare*, formed from *strages* as *plantare* is formed from *planta*. The phonetic development **stragere* > *estragar* is doubtless regular, being exactly paralleled by that of *plagare* > *llagar*.

2. *Sesgar* 'to cut on the bias', *sesgo* 'oblique'.

The type **sesecare* 'to cut apart', proposed by me in the *Publications of the Modern Language Association of America* 20. 343, after having been accepted by Meyer-Lübke, *Romanisches etymologisches Wörterbuch*, has been attackt by Leo Spitzer, *Revista de filología española* 13. 116, on the sole ground that the prefix *se-* is no longer productive in Romance. Spitzer tries to show a connection between *sesgar* and **sessicare*, a type postulated by Meyer-Lübke to account for Old Spanish *sessegar* 'sich setzen, sich niederlassen', and by Meyer-Lübke taken as the source of Spanish *sosegar* 'to quiet'. I shall discuss below both *sosegar* and **sessicare*.

On the formal side, we should note in the postulated development **sessicare* > OS *sessegar* > S *sesgar* the suspicious dropping of a syllable between the old and modern Spanish period. Spitzer cites, to be sure, one similar-looking series, *vindicare* > *vendegar* > *vengar*; but this comparison suggests phonological and morphological queries. Would **sessicare*, a late formation, show the same treatment of the second vowel as *vindicare*, an ancient word? Is not *vendegar* (the occurrence of which I am unable to verify) a semi-learned rather than a popular development? In Menéndez Pidal's *Manual* 65$_1$, 133, I find *vengar* given as the popular, *vindicar* as the learned derivative of *vindicare*. If *vendegar* is the regular Old Spanish form of *vindicare*, as Spitzer seems to think, why is it not to be found in Meyer-Lübke's *Romanische Grammatik* or *Romanisches etymologisches Wörterbuch*?

On the semantic side, the suggested etymology leaves even more to be explained. Spitzer supposes that the original sense of *sesgar* was 'to set', mentions Spanish *sesga* 'gore', compares the German phrase 'einen Lappen (Flicken) einsetzen', but fails to attack seriously the problem of showing that the meaning 'to set' might naturally shift to that of 'to cut across'. To be sure, *sesga* 'gore' is to be associated with the verb *sesgar* or with the adjective *sesgo*, but it is readily interpreted as meaning etymologically 'a cutting' or 'an oblique piece'.

Spitzer suggests that the type **sesecare*, which has always displeased him, might be eliminated in the interest of reducing the number of etyma in the Romance dictionary. However, it is phonetically perfect, and gives a meaning quite close to the meanings of the Spanish derivatives assigned to it. Its formation being paralleled by that of *secedere, secernere, secludere, semovere, seponere* and various other Latin words, the linguistic facts shown seem to me to indicate that the word **sesecare* probably existed in ancient Latin.

The type **sexicare*, formed from an assumed participle **sexus* for *sectus* was suggested by Ullrich in the *Zeitschrift für romanische Philologie* 4. 383. Meyer-Lübke, *REW* 592, calls the formation of **sexus* improbable. However, Ullrich cited no less than 13 variants like *fixus* beside *fictus*, etc.[1] While the formation **sexicare* seems to me justifiable, its short vowel makes it phonetically a less desirable type than **sesecare*; and the meaning of the latter word is also somewhat closer to that of the Spanish verb.

3. *Simado* 'deep' (of lands), *sima* 'abyss'.

Baist, *Zeitschrift für rom. Phil.* 5. 563, derived *sima* from Greek σῑμός 'eingebogen, hohl, ansteigend'. This etymology has recently been rejected by Meyer-Lübke, *REW*, defended by Persson, *Eranos* 20. 80,[2] and contested by Spitzer, *Rev. de fil. esp.* 23.117, who proposes instead the type **sedimen*, a base recorded by Meyer-Lübke, following Salvioni (*Z. f. rom. Phil.* 22. 174) as the etymon for Old Italian *sedime*, 'Untergrund'. However, Spitzer realizes that **sedimen* would rather have produced **seimbre*, irregularly **simbre* in Spanish. This **simbre* he sees in Spanish *cimbre* 'subterranean gallery'. I am willing to admit a degree of probability in this one feature of Spitzer's etymology. But it is much harder to follow him when

---

[1] *Fartus farsus, fixus fictus, fluxus fluctus, frictus frixus, indultus indulsus, mersus mertus, emulsus emulctus, pulsus pultus, sartus sarsus, scriptus scripsus, tensus tentus, tertus tersus, tortus torsus.*

[2] In this article Persson shows conclusively that σῑμός meant originally 'bent', 'concave', and that its use in the sense of 'snub' is a secondary specialization.

he suggests that *sedimen* may also have developt into *sima*, comparing Old Spanish *sija* beside *seija* < *sedilia*, and Spanish *grama* < *gramen*, both irregular developments. On the whole, the irregularities presented by the etymology are so great that it may be said to rest merely on the meaning of the etymon indicated by the Old Italian word, and on a slight resemblance in forms.

The Greek adjective σῑμός means not only 'snub', 'bent upwards', but also, according to unmistakable lexicographic evidence shown in the Greek dictionaries, 'hollow', 'concave'. This essential fact establisht the semantic basis for Baist's etymology. Meyer-Lübke rejects not σιμός, which, in accordance with his usual practice when dealing with Greek-Latin etyma, he does not distinctly mention, but the attested *simus*, defined as 'aufwärts gebogen, platt', which he declares 'begriffllich nicht möglich'. Now is it not fair to assume, notwithstanding this summary treatment and Spitzer's opposition in the interest of the etymon *sedimen*, that *simus* had not only the meaning 'snub' but also that of 'hollow', in Latin as in Greek? A considerable number of Greek words which have descended into the Romance languages are not in the Latin dictionary at all, yet both the form and the meaning which they must have had in Vulgar Latin are regarded as known. Leaving out of account doubtful bases and borrowings from middle and modern Greek, I find 115 Greek etyma among the 182 Greek words listed by Meyer-Lübke on pages 1072 and 1073 of the *REW* as not recorded in the same form and meaning in George's *Lateinisch-deutsches Wörterbuch*. For example, the etymon of French *plat* and its congeners is given as Greek *plattus*, 'flach'. Now, the existence of *plattus* in Vulgar Latin is inferred from the form of the Romance words, and it is generally connected, for example by Schwan-Behrens, *Grammaire de l'ancien français*[3] 123, with Greek πλατύς, which, however, means essentially 'broad', only secondarily and occasionally '*flat*'. When we find *platys* attested *once* in Pliny[3] with the meaning 'broad', not in that of 'flat', and note that the word means 'broad' in modern Greek, are we to abandon the etymology unless we can find the meaning 'flat' attested in Latin? Certainly not; yet such a procedure would be rather analogous to that of Meyer-Lübke and Spitzer in accepting for the Latin *simus*, obviously borrowed from the Greek, only that meaning which happens to be attested in Latin.

Starting, therefore, from the form *simus*, assumed to mean 'hollow' in Vulgar Latin as in Greek, I posit the verb *simare* 'to hollow', the past participle of which accounts for the adjective *simado* 'deep' (of land). *Sima* 'abyss', properly 'hollow', may be taken either from the adjective *simus* or from *simare* as a postverbal.

[3] Pliny 26.5.58: nervus qui *platys* appellatur.

4. *Sosegar* 'to pacify', *sosiego* 'tranquillity'.

The verb is often derived from **sessicare*, but the *o* presents enormous difficulty, as all who have studied Spanish phonology will at once admit.[4] The base **sessicare*, I will note in passing, should not be associated with the intransitive verb *sedere*, but must be formed from the noun *sessus*, 'seat'.

Sosegar is, I am convinced, another word. I derive it from the base **insulsicare*, a type formed like **albicare*, **amaricare*, etc., to which I assign the primary meaning 'to stupefy', whence—perhaps originally as a medical term—'to quiet'. Cf. Spanish *soso* 'flavorless', 'stupid', < Latin *insulsus* 'flavorless', 'stupid'.

According to Crouch, *Encyclopaedia Britannica* 1. 207, there is abundant evidence to show that the use of anesthetics is a practice of great antiquity.

The diphthong in the strest syllable of *sosiego* is evidently due to the attraction of the verbal forms like *sosiega*, where it results from the analogy of verbs having a short *e* in the stem, which develop the diphthong regularly. Cf. Menéndez Pidal, *Manual* 229, where the following examples of this shift are given, among others: *siembran, piensa, friega, pliega, riega, nieva*.

[4] Körting, *Lateinisch-romanisches, Wörterbuch*[3], favors Storm's etymon **subsedicare*, which Meyer-Lübke, *REW*, rejects on phonetic grounds, preferring Michaelis' type **sessicare* (influenced by *sub*),—likewise a very irregular etymology.

VIII

ADDITIONAL NOTES ON SPANISH *ESTRAGAR*, *SESGAR* *SIMADO (SIMA)*, *SOSEGAR*

Since the publication of my Spanish Etymologies in *Language* (Vol. V, no. 1), I have received from Professor Jakob Jud of the University of Zurich and Professor Adolph Zauner of the University of Graz communications in which they comment on certain points in the four etymologies advocated by me in that article. Their comments having led me to study the words anew, I now add the following notes on the points raised by these scholars, whose views I generally quote, for the sake of accuracy, in their own terms.

1. *Estragar*, 'to ruin', 'to spoil', < **stragare* (formed from *strages*).

Supporting the formation of **stragare* from *strages*, Jud compares Latin *propagare* beside *propages*, showing a verb in *-gare* derived from a noun in *-ges*, "à moins que *propages* ne soit postérieur à *propagare*. En tout cas il faut admettre un dérivé déjà latin...."

Zauner comments on this etymology: "You may be right for *estragar* ... **Stragicare* [Meyer-Lübke's etymon] would not have given **estraigar*, I think, but **estracar*; cf. **figicare *ficcare*."

2. *Sesgar*, 'to cut on the bias', < **sesecare*, 'to cut apart.'

Zauner remarks: "As to *sesgar*, the fact that the prefix *se-* was evidently of little use in popular Latin (of the words you quote none has remained in Rom. Lang.) seems to be a serious obstacle to your etymology."

In reply to this objection, I have to say that the list of words containing the prefix *se-* which I cited in my article was professedly incomplete. It seemed to me that if the existence of the word **sesecare* in classic Latin was rendered fairly probable, its postulation as a Romance etymon was justified. However, I am now actually able to mention one Latin verb compounded with *se-* which has survived, namely *separare*, 'to disjoin', which became **seperare* in late Vulgar Latin and then developt regularly into Old French *sevrer*, 'to sever', French *sevrer*, 'to wean'. I call attention to the close resemblance in form and meaning between *separare*, 'to separate' and the postulated **sesecare* 'to cut apart'. I submit that if the proposed derivation of *sesgar* from **sesecare* is to be rejected for the sole reason that words containing the prefix *se-* do not seem to have survived in the Romance languages, then the derivation of *sevrer* from *separare* may

Previously unpublished.

properly be regarded as suspicious—a manifest absurdity, the survival of *separare* in *sevrer* being of course unquestionable.

3. *Simado*, 'deep' (of lands), < **sīmātum*, 'hollowed' p. p. of **sīmare*, 'to hollow', formed from *sīmus*, **'hollow'*, Greek οἱμός, 'hollow'. *Sima*, 'abyss' (postverbal noun, or substantivized adjective).

Jud remarks: "*Sedimen* ne veut pas dire *Untergrund* dans l'Italie du Nord, mais le terrain sur lequel une maison est bâtie. Ce *sedimen* n'a rien à faire avec *sima*." In making this statement, Jud apparently assumes that the words listed by Meyer-Lübke as connected with *sedimen*, namely "canav. *sim* 'Hof', *simp* 'Bauernhof', friaul. *sedim*," are actually derived from that word—an assumption the phonetic basis of which is not obvious to me. However, it may be noted that Jud here explicitly agrees with me in rejecting Spitzer's connection of the base *sedimen* with Spanish *sima*. Zauner likewise remarks: "You may be right for ... *simado*."

4. *Sosegar*, 'to quiet' < **insulsicare*, 'to stupefy'.

On this etymology, Jud comments as follows: "*Insulsicare*, possible au point de vue phonétique, n'est-il pas un peu étonnant au point de vue de la sémantique? *Albicare* c'est blanchoyer, *amaricare* c'est rendre amer, *insulsicare* ne serait-ce pas rendre fade? De plus le verbe existe en prov. mod.—*souscà*, rêver, réfléchir, méditer (cf. Mistral); Vasconcellos, Estudos de phil. mir. 2, 215 cite aussi un ancien portug. *sessegar*, Nunes *assessego*, Carolina Michaelis Miranda 890 *assessego*. C'est un problême à reprendre."

Zauner says in this connection: "Of the bases proposed for *sosegar* none can be considered, I think, as satisfactory (nor can yours). It is probable the *i* in the suffix would have been dropped and the semantic development of **insulsicare* that you suppose seems to me artificial. But of course that is a matter of personal taste."

I will endeavor to answer these objections to the derivation of *sosegar* from **insulsicare*. Turning first to the phonetic development, I find that while Jud admits as possible the assumed phonology, Zauner thinks the pretonic vowel should have dropt. Now, the form which **insulsicare* took in late Vulgar Latin may of course be set down as **sulsicare*, inasmuch as *insulsus* (=**sulsus*) became *soso* in Spanish. The development of **sulsicare* into *sosegar* is quite analogous to that of **albicare* into *albegar*. The assumption of a semi-learned phonetic development is therefore unnecessary, tho possible. I have already suggested that **insulsicare* may have been a medical term.

The Portuguese words cited by Jud are in my opinion plainly shown by their form to be from another stem; that is, from the **sessicare* posited by Michaelis and Meyer-Lübke. As for the Provençal word *souscà*, which Jud identifies with *sosegar*, it is derived by Mistral from *suspicare*, 'to suspect'. This etymology seems quite probable to me tho it is not even mentioned by Körting or Meyer-Lübke, who fail to register the Provençal word giving only the obviously cognate Old French *souschier*, 'argwöhnen.' The derivation of *souscà* from *suspicare* is phonetically regular, and the meanings, 'rêver', 'réfléchir', 'méditer' are clearly allied with that of 'to suspect'. However, the Provençal word has, according to Mistral, also the meanings 'sangloter', 'souffler', 'attendre', which deserve further study. Possibly these senses, so remote from that of 'to suspect', indicate that there is another *souscà* from a different etymon, as yet undiscovered.

Insulsus certainly meant 'stupid' as well as 'insipid' in classic Latin. In view of this fact, it is hard to see how the postulation of the meaning 'stupefy' for *insulsicare can be regarded as astonishing; particularly when we notice that the Latin synonym of *insulsus*, namely *stupidus*, meant not only 'stupid' but also 'struck senseless'; and that the English word 'senseless' means not only 'silly' but also 'unconscious'. The postulation of a shift of meaning from that of 'to stupefy (by soporifics)' into that of 'to lull', 'to quiet', seems to me entirely legitimate, indeed rather simple.[1]

I have to acknowledge the courtesy shown me by Professors Jud and Zauner in transmitting to me their interesting and suggestive remarks on my article.

[1] The above argument seems to meet also the analogous objections to the etymon *insulsicare raised by H. B. Richardson, *Etymological Vocabulary to the Libro de buen amor*, 1930, *s. v.*

IX

SPANISH *BAZO*; *CERDO*; *EMPACHAR*; *ESQUEJAR*; *ESTROPEAR*; *ESTRUJAR*

1. Spanish *bazo*, OS *baço* 'yellowish brown'; *bazo* 'spleen'.

Körting's **vasium*, suggested as the etymon of *bazo* 'spleen', would doubtless have developt exactly like *basium* > *beso*. The **bombacius* for *bombyceus* 'of cotton or silk', suggested by Diez, accepted by Horning[1], but doubted by Meyer-Lübke, may be said to present considerable phonetic and semantic difficulty.

I propose to derive *bazo* 'yellowish brown' from a Latinized form of Greek βαθύς 'deep', which in Roman and Byzantine Greek means also 'deep-colored'. Pape[2] gives one example of the meaning 'tiefdunkel' from Aelian (3rd century A.D.). Sophocles[3] mentions three passages in which βαθύς is used as an adjective of color: Aelian V. H. 6. 6, with ὄψις 'dark appearance'; Gregory of Nyssa (4th century A.D.) 3. 1081 A, with ἀλουργίς 'dark purple robe'; Lydus (6th century A. D.) 178.15, with ραφή 'dark dye'. The Thesaurus Graecus adduces also similar citations from Charito (4th century A.D.) and from the grammarian Hesychius (5th century A.D.), with comment.

In The Phonology of Gallic Clerical Latin[4] I have shown that Greek θ was pronounced in Latin as *ts* in the tenth century and later. The assumption of a late Latin **bathus* with the *th* pronounced as *ts* is therefore justified. One Spanish word, *tio* < θεῖος, shows the earlier Latin pronunciation of θ as *t*; but the corresponding word in Italian, *zio*, represents the later Latin pronunciation of θ.

I derive *bazo* 'spleen' from the same source, on the supposition that the original meaning was 'deep-colored organ'. 'The human spleen ... is of a dull purple color ...'[5]

2. Spanish *cerdo* 'hog'. Meyer-Lübke, rightly rejecting the etymon *sordidus*, advocated by Diez (which would have become **suerdio*), is inclined to favor derivation[6] from *cerda* 'bristle', tracing the latter Spanish

---

[1] Z. f. rom. Phil. 27. 347.
[2] Griechisch-lat. Handwörterbuch, s. v.
[3] Greek Lexicon of the Roman and Byzantine periods, s. v.
[4] Harvard dissertation of 1902, publisht 1907, p. 81.
[5] Encyclopaedia Brittanica[14] 7. 707.
[6] This etymology is due to D. S. Blondheim, in Studies in Honor of A. Marshall Elliott 1. 245–50.

word back to a supposed contamination between *cirrus* 'tuft of hair' and *saeta* 'arrow'.

This assumed contamination seems to me extremely unlikely; and even on the semantic side the etymology lacks plausibility, in that the meaning 'hog' is probably antecedent to that of 'bristle', rather than the reverse.

According to Diez, Larramendi derived *cerdo* from Basque *cherria* 'swine'; which in López' dictionary appears as *zerri, txerri*; but these forms, the base of which ends in *i*, are not obviously related to the Spanish word. However, in this connection I quote the view of Mr. E. H. Tuttle, who writes as follows:

> An older form of Bask *zerri* seems to be the source of *cerda, cerdo*, just as an older form of *ezker* is the source of *izquierdo*. The change of the final vowel to -*a* and -*o* has a parallel in *paloma, palomo*, beside Latin *palumbem*. The *r* of *ezker* stands for *rr* (as in the derivative *ezkerreta*); *izquierdo* implies a change of *rd* to *rr* in Bask. The sound *s*, written *z*, seems to have come from an older *ts* in Bask, parallel with Spanish θ from *ts*.

I suggest that *cerdo* may be a postverbal formation from Vulgar Latin *seritare, an already postulated frequentative of *serere* 'to sow, beget produce'. The only phonetic difficulty involved is the assumed substitution of *c* for the initial *s*, which however is paralleled by *cedazo* < *setaceum, cerrar* < *serare, zueco* < *soccum*, and the like, on which I refer to Menéndez Pidal[7], who believes that words showing this irregularity come from Andalusia.

The designation of the hog by a term meaning 'procreation', 'production', or product', is not unlike the designation of cattle in Spain as *ganado*, literally 'gain'.

Cerda 'bristle' is related to *cerdo* 'hog' as *vaca, becerro* 'sole leather', 'calf-skin' are related to *vaca, becerro* 'cow', 'calf'. The variation in gender is similar to that seen in *cardo* 'thistle' *carda* 'teasle', *cargo* 'loading' *carga* 'load', and the like.

3. Spanish *empachar* 'to impede,' 'to embarrass'; *empacho* 'embarrassment'.

The other Romance words which obviously have to be considered in connection with the Spanish words are, in the first place, Rumanian *împedicà*, Old Italian *impedicare*, Old French *empeechier*, and Provençal *empedegar*, which are plainly derived from Latin *impedicare*, the Old French and Provençal forms being semi-learned; and secondly, Provençal *empachar*, Catalan *empaitar*, Portuguese *empachar*, Italian *impacciare*, which must be from the same etymon as Spanish *empachar*. Körting, following Diez, connects them with the obscure stem *bag*, assuming the sense-development

---

[7] Manual de gram. hist.[5] 99.

'pack in', 'stuff full', 'check', hinder'. This etymology is rightly rejected on phonetic grounds by Meyer-Lübke, who, following in part other writers, attempts to derive the entire second group of Romance words from Old French *empeechier*. This theory shows two phonetic weaknesses: the change of OF *ee* to *a* in Spanish, etc., is anomalous; and Catalan *empaitar* has to be explained as an analogical form.

I derive the second group from a Vulgar Latin **impattiare* 'to impede', formed much like *im-ped-icare*; that is, from VL **patta* 'paw', by the use of the popular verbal suffix *-iare*. The development of *tty* into Spanish *ch*, Italian *cc*, etc., appears not to contradict any establisht phonetic rule, although exact parallels are wanting. In the absence of establisht VL words containing *tty* it may not be amiss to point to the *ch* in Spanish *capacho* beside Old Spanish *capaço* < *cappaceum*; *ricacho* beside Portuguese *ricaço*; *hornacho* besides OS *hornazo* < *furnaceum*; although in these cases we have VL etyma with *cy* instead of *ty*, and the variant reflexes are not well understood.

I of course derive Spanish *despachar* analogously from **de-ex-patt-iare*.

4. Spanish *esquejar* 'to make cuttings', *esqueje* 'cutting', *desquejar* 'to make cuttings from sprouts .

In attempting to etymologize these words, we should consider Catalan *esqueixar*, *esqueix*, with analogous meanings, and Provençal *esquissa*, which according to Mistral means 'déchirer, rompre'. Mistral lists as dialectic variants of *esquissa* the forms *esquiéussa*, *esquinsa*, *escouissa*, *escouicha*. However, as is indicated by Körting and Meyer-Lübke, *esquinsa* is from **exquintiare*. Furthermore, the other variants are likewise from a different base; that is, from a stem containing a short *o*; and I suggest their derivation from the type **excostiare*, meaning presumably 'to cut out the ribs', which seems to account for them all regularly.

As for *esquejar*, Körting correctly rejects Vogel's **de-ex-scidiare* on the ground that *sci* cannot become *que* in Spanish. The Spanish word does not appear in Meyer-Lübke's index, and he does not mention it among the derivatives of *schidia* 'splinter', which include Italian *scheggia* 'splinter'. Others, however, including the etymologists of the Spanish Academy, as evidenced by its Diccionario, have not hesitated to connect *esqueje* with *schidia*; but the phonetic assumption involved is quite difficult, since intervocalic *dy* regularly becomes *y* in Spanish. Derivation of *esquejar* from the Italian verb *scheggiare* 'to splinter' would seem attractive but for the existence of the Catalan and Provençal forms, which cannot be obtained from a stem containing a voiced consonant, and which seem to demand a base containing the group *sty*.

I therefore propose to derive the verb *esquejar* from the type **schistiare* 'to split', a Vulgar Latin formation from the attested *schistos* (= Greek σχιστός). This *schistos* is a technical term used by the elder Pliny in the sense of 'schistose', 'fissile'. Pliny also uses the adjective to modify the noun *lac*, the combination meaning 'curdled milk'; and to modify the noun *caepo*, the phrase designating a variety of onion. The word thus seems to have had a popular status in late Latin.

Ford[8] indicates that the phonetic group *sty* regularly develops into Old Spanish *x*, modern Spanish *j*. The phonetic development postulated for Provençal *esquissa* and Catalan *esqueixar* likewise agrees with Grandgent's phonological statements.[9]

5. Spanish *estropear* 'to cripple'.

In connection with this Spanish verb, we should mention Old Spanish *estorpar*, Portuguese *estropear*, Italian *storpiare*, *stroppiare*, French *estropier*, all meaning 'to cripple'.

Diez's etymon *extorpidare, containing the stem of the adjective *torpidus*, is evidently inadmissible. Körting suggests connection with *stroppus* 'strap', assuming the meaning 'to cut a piece of leather into straps, thereby making it unsightly', 'to ruin'. This etymology would seem to require further support on the semantic side. It is not even mentioned by Meyer-Lübke, who doubtfully suggests derivation from *stuprare* 'to dishonor'.

I propose to derive Old Spanish *estorpar*, *destorpar* from *exturpare, *de-exturpare rather than from *disturpare, the etymon suggested by Cornu.[10] For the modern Spanish and Portuguese verbs I confidently postulate the type *exturpidiare. It is known that the prefix *ex-* is used to emphasize the meaning of Latin verbs, as in *elaudare*, *evastare*, *exacerbare*, *exaugere*, *educere*, *exaltare*, *excoriare*, etc. The commonness of the suffix *-idiare* is clearly indicated by Menéndez Pidal.[11] Italian *storpiare* represents the type *exturpiare, with an irregular open *o* in the stem-accented forms. Popular Italian *stroppiare* shows the further anomalies of metathesis and double *p*. French *estropier* is borrowed from the Italian, as Meyer-Lübke states.

On the semantic side, the Latin dictionary gives us *turpare* 'to make ugly, defile, pollute, disfigure, deform'.

6. Spanish *estrujar* 'to squeeze out'; *truja* 'olive bin in oil mills'.

The verb is connected by Diez with Latin *torculum* 'press', which by a metathesis gives French *treuil*, Provençal *trolh*, Catalan *troll*. The assumption of a Vulgar Latin verb *extroculare may thus seem reasonable. But

---

[8] Old Spanish Sibilants 120.
[9] Old Provençal Phonology 67.
[10] Romania 13. 300.
[11] Manual[5] 287.

such a type should have developt into *estrojar* in Spanish; and there appears to be no further evidence for the existence of a type **extroculare*.

I suggest that *estrujar* may be from a type **extrusulare*, a diminutive from **extrusare* 'to thrust out', a recognized Vulgar Latin verb. The noun *truja* seems to be a postverbal, with the prefix dropt. Other VL types containing the group *sl* are hard to quote, but it seems possible that this group becomes *j* in Spanish.

X

SPANISH *ABARCA*; *CISCAR*; *¡OLE!*

1. *Abarca* 'a kind of footwear of rawhide, covering the sole, the toes and most of the foot, and fastened with cords or straps over the instep and ankle'.[1]

According to a traditional etymology accepted by Diez and advocated by Baist[2], this word is derived from Basque *abarka* 'shoe'. But Schuchardt[3] has declared the Basque word a borrowing from the Spanish, rejecting Astarloa's analysis of the Basque word into *abar* 'branch' and *kia* 'thing', and deriving the Spanish word from Latin *barca* 'boat'. The meaning 'wooden' assigned by Diez to Basque *abar* is not confirmed by the Basque-Spanish-French dictionary of R. M. de Azkue (Bilbao, 1905), and appears to rest merely on a doubtful semantic assumption. Furthermore, of course, the Spanish word does not designate a wooden but a leather shoe. Meyer-Lübke, wavering between the two rival etymologies in the second edition[4] follows Baist in the third, objecting to Latin *barca* for the reason that it will not account for the initial syllable of Sp. *abarca*.[5] This phonetic objection is valid; for while various Spanish words show an incorporated *Arabic* article, sometimes reduced to *a-*, as in *azote* < Ar.(*al*)*saut*, one looks in vain for Latin words similarly treated.

I derive *abarca* from the Sp. verb *abarcar* 'to clasp, embrace, contain' or its Latin etymon *abbrachicare. For morphological parallels I refer to the scores of similar postverbals indicated by Meyer-Lübke.[6] The closest semantic parallels in his list are *alza* 'piece of leather put around the last to make the shoe wider' from *alzar* 'to raise'; *cerca* 'fence' from *cercar* 'surround'; *ensancha* 'extention' from *ensanchar* 'to widen'.

Abarca thus meant originally 'that which clasps, embraces, contains' the foot, as distinguisht from common sandals, which consist of a sole strapt to the foot. Another morphological and semantic parallel may be seen in English *Oxford tie* 'a low shoe laced or tied over the instep'.

[1] Spanish Academy, Diccionario.
[2] Zeitschrift f. rom. Phil. 32. 43.
[3] Zeitschrift f. rom. Phil. 15. 115.
[4] Rom.Et.Wb.², index, *s. v.*
[5] The objection to the transfer of meaning 'boat' > 'clasp-shoe', adumbrated by Meyer-Lübke, will hardly hold in view of northern Italian *barka* 'large shoe' (Meyer-Lübke³ s.v. *barca*) and colloquial Sp. *lancha* 'clumsy shoe', lit. 'boat'.
[6] Rom. Gram. 2.445.

2. *Ciscar*, familiar, transitive 'to dirty anything', reflexive, 'to loosen or evacuate the bowels' has not yet been etymologized by lexicographers. It seems to be connected with Sp. *cisco* 'fine coal', figurative and familiar; 'uproar, row, hubbub'.

I believe *cisco* to be a postverbal derivative with the original meaning 'dirt'; *ciscarse* to be derived from *phӯsicare sē 'to doctor oneself', this giving readily the meaning 'to loosen or evacuate the bowels', which I take to be the original meaning of the verb. In OS, *físico* means physician and the noun *maestro* is accompanied by the verb *amaestrar* 'to teach'. It is thus plain that *phӯsicare sē may naturally have developt the meaning 'to doctor oneself' in OS.

In the substitution of *c* for *f* in the initial syllable we have a case of 'acoustic equivalence', on which I refer to Menéndez Pidal.[7] The examples cited by him include vulgar *Celipe, Cilomena, zorro* for *Felipe, Filomena, forro*, and are followed by 'etc.', indicating the commonness of the phenomenon.

3. *¡Ole!* an injection for encouraging and applauding; 2. m. A certain Andalusian dance; 3. Tune for this dance.'

The derivation of the word from Arabic *wallah* 'by God', indicated in the Spanish Academy's dictionary, may be rejected without discussion on phonetic grounds.

I suggest derivation from Lat. *hōc illi* 'this for him!', an interjection which may have been used originally in the bull-ring, accompanied by the throwing of presents to bull-fighters, which has probably always been a common practice. A semantic parallel may be seen in OF *o il* 'that he (does)', modern French *oui* 'yes'; OF *o el* in answer to questions with impersonal verbs: *pluet? o el* 'Is it raining? Yes.'[8]

For the phonology, compare Sp. *pero* < *per hōc*, *le* < *illi*. That *hoc* had a long vowel in some regions is definitely stated by Grandgent.[9] It is to be assumed that the two vocables develop separately, without coalescence in Vulgar Latin.

[7] Gram. hist.³ 165 (1929).
[8] Tobler, Vermischte Beiträge 1.1.
[9] Vulgar Latin 69.

XI
MORE ON *CISCAR*

Max J. Luria[1], contesting the derivation of Spanish *ciscar* 'to dirty', *cisco* 'charcoal dust' from Latin *physicare se* 'to doctor oneself', suggested by me[2], attempts to connect the words with an adjective *ciniscus formed from Latin *cinis* 'ashes'. He points out that in an article quoted by Körting[3], C. Michaelis de Vasconcellos[4] derived Portuguese *cisco* 'charcoal dust' from *cinisculus* 'a little ashes', and that Meyer-Lübke[5] questioned this etymology on phonological grounds. Meyer-Lübke actually says specifically, that the Portuguese *i* presents difficulty (if the word is referred to *cinisculus*).

Luria is apparently right in opposing the derivation of *ciscar* from *physicare*, since it should probably be admitted that the assumption of a phonetic confusion of *c-* and *f-* cannot well be extended to cover the Portuguese initial *c-* = *s-*. However, his article is patently weak on the constructive side, since the series *cĭnĭscu (sic) > *cĭnĭscu[6] (by dissimilation) > *cīns'cu > *cisco*, cannot be taken seriously until the assumed irregular stress on the suggested *cĭnĭscu has been justified, and the alleged dissimilation of $ĭ + ĭ$ to $ī + ĭ$ has been supported by reasonable analogies, and the assumed disappearance of the *n* in Spanish has been made credible. The definitions and semantic argument which he presents fail to demonstrate that the source of the Hispanic group must have meant 'ashen'; and it seems that the type *ciniscus ought to have become *cenesco in Spanish. To be sure, it might have become *cesco in Portuguese (cf. *sinistrum* > *sestro*). If a base *cinīscu were taken, it would still fail to account for the Spanish forms except on the supposition—unlikely in view of the difference in meaning between the Spanish and Portuguese verbs— that the Spanish words are borrowed from the Portuguese. Furthermore, the antiquity of the suffix—*īscus* is doubtful: Meyer-Lübke[7] mentions *arenisco*, *blanquisco*, which are not recorded in Cejador[8], *barberisco*, *morisco*

---

[1] Lang. 13.315–7 (1937) and ibid. 14.65 (1938) for correction of misprint.
[2] Lang. 8.143 (1932).
[3] Körting, Latein-romanisches Wb., no. 2195.
[4] Revista lusitana 3.140 (1895).
[5] REW 1929.
[6] See note 1.
[7] Gramm. des langues rom., II, §520.
[8] Voc. med. español.

Previously unpublished.

(mentioned by Cejador as occurring in the *Cid*), *levantisco*, remarking that the *i* of the last three words shows that they originated in Middle Latin.

I am now inclined to refer the Hispanic group to a Vulgar Latin **cīsicare* 'to cut or prune off', 'to clear (timber)', whence 'cleanings', particularly 'charcoal cleanings', 'slack'. The meaning of Spanish *ciscar* 'to dirty', *ciscarse* 'to move the bowels' may be original—'to clean out the bowels' or (less probably) postnominal, from *cisco* 'charcoal dust', on the assumption that this sense shifted to that of 'dirt'. The semantic shift 'prune off', 'clear (timber)' > 'clean out (the bowels)' seems to present merely different phases of 'cleaning'. The Portuguese verb, according to Coelho⁹, means 'to clear, from land which is to be plowed, unburned twigs and branches'; and the regional Portuguese *semses* 'pine-needles', 'sweepings' given by Meyer-Lübke¹⁰ following Michaelis¹¹, may also be derived from the notion of 'cleanings'. The meaning 'hubbub' assumed by Spanish *cisco* in the phrase *meter cisco en una reunión*¹², which Luria connects with the figurative sense of Latin *cinis* 'destruction, ruin, annihilation', is merely a modern development of the meaning 'charcoal dust', quite analogous to the figurative meaning of English *dust*¹³.

The base **cīsicare*, which I now postulate, may be connected with Latin *caedere* '*to cut*', thru the participle *caesus* > *cesus* — **cīsus*, the stem vowel having been modified to agree with that of the participles of the numerous compounds of *caedere*: *decisus* (*decidere* 'cut away'), *excisus* (*excidere* 'cut out'), *incisus* (*incidere* 'cut into'), *intercisus* (*intercidere* 'cut asunder') *occisus* (*occidere* 'strike down'), *praecisus* (praecidere 'cut off in front'), *recisus* (*recidere* 'cut away'), *succisus* (*succidere* 'cut off below').

The survival of the stem *cīs-* 'cut' in Vulgar Latin is, furthermore, attested by such Romance reflexes as French *enciser* < **incisare*, Italian *inchischiare* < **incisulare*, so that the postulation of a VL **cīsicare*, containing the common suffix *-icare*, cannot easily be dismisst as an improbable formation.

⁹ Diccionario manual etymologico da lingua portugeza.
¹⁰ [I can not locate this reference. U. T. H.]
¹¹ See note 10.
¹² Pequeño Larousse, under *cisco*.
¹³ [Professor Rice left a note among his papers in which he referred to the article by Leo Spitzer on *cisco, ciscar* in Lang. 14.147-8 (1938). Rice thought that Spitzer's comparison with **cisc-* 'peer' was not needed to explain the evolution of meaning. He added further that the Portuguese sense 'to clear up unburned twigs' could come easily from the meanings 'dust' and 'clean'. Rice also remarked upon Norman P. Sacks's article on the same forms, in Hispanic Review 6.264 (1938). He did not agree that the Spanish words came from the Portuguese. Rice thought that Sacks's *cinīsculus* for *cinĭsculus* was an unlikely form. U. T. H.]

XII

PROVENÇAL *ESCACHA*; ITALIAN *FRIZZARE, PAGGIO*; OLD FRENCH *PUIRIER*; PROVENÇAL *TROBAR*

1. Provençal *escacha, escaicha, escaissa*, 'break with the teeth', 'break', 'tear', 'bite' is not mentioned by Meyer-Lübke. The forms *escacha, escaissa* seem to be regular reflexes of *excoactare, *excoactiare 'to smash', the *ai* in *escaicha* being due to the attraction of *escaissa*. Meyer-Lübke does mention French *écacher* 'to smash' along with French *cacher* 'to hide' as a doubtful derivative of *coacticare. These French words seem to be Provençal loanwords from*[*ex*]*coactare*. Provençal *quichà* 'to press', 'to pinch' must have some other source.

2. Italian *frizzare* 'to smart' < *frīctiare : *frīctus* : *frīgo* 'to roast'. The word was derived by Diez from *frictiare : *frĭctus* : *frĭco* 'to rub'; but the latter etymology presents phonetic irregularity as well as semantic difficulty, and is not repeated by Meyer-Lübke,[1] who omits the word. The phonetic development *frīctiare > *frizzare* may be regular. In *rizzare, dirizzare* we have, to be sure, a voiceless *zz* from *cty* (< **rectiare,* *directiare), but the examples hardly establish a phonetic law. The variant treatment of *cty* in *rizzare* and *frizzare* seems to show a regional divergence.

3. Italian *paggio* 'young servant', French *page* 'page' was derived by Diez from Greek παιδίον 'boy', on the supposition that it was brought from Byzantium during the Crusades. Meyer-Lübke, in his Romanische Grammatik,[2] more plausibly assumed that *padium was an *early* Greek loanword, the non-appearance of which in Latin writing is a mere accident. Still, as no other early Greek loanword showing this phonetic development has survived in Romance, the etymology must be declared quite doubtful. Meyer-Lübke himself, in the third edition of his Rom. Etym. Wb., doubts the derivation of *paggio* from παιδίον on the ground that the word is older in French than in Italian. Now it is true that the word is attested in French as early as the thirteenth century; but recognition of that fact does not necessitate the abandonment of the common assumption that the word came to France from Italy, as the direction of vocabulary loans often has to be made out from the phonology of the words rather than from the dates of their appearance in writing. On this principle, Meyer-Lübke, for

[1] Rom. Etym. Wb.²,³
[2] 1. 32.

example, admits the derivation of Old Spanish *testa* from Catalan *testa* 'head';[3] and the derivation of Old Italian *gorgia* from French *gorge* 'throat'.[4]

I propose to derive the Italian word from Vulgar Latin **pageus*, a type parallel with *pagensis* > French *pays* 'country', formed from *pagus* + *-eus* instead of *-ensis*. Meyer-Lübke[5] gives about forty examples of the use of the suffix *-eus*, and says that substantivized adjectives (like *lineum* : *linum*) are numerous. The Italian phonology assumed is regular.

After having decided to present this etymology, I found a similar theory set forth in his dictionary by Littré, who mentions Low Latin *pagius* 'page', and postulates the Vulgar Latin type *pagius*.

4. Old French *puirier* 'to hand on', 'to offer' was derived by Diez from *porrigere* 'to reach'; but, as Meyer-Lübke indicates,[6] this is not clear. In view of the existence of the Old French particle *por*, *puer*, Provençal *por*, *pore*, noticed by Diez[7] in compounds like Provençal *por gitar* 'to throw away', and by him derived from Latin *porro*, I propose to connect *puirier* with the type **porriare* : *porro* + *-iare*. This formation is analogous to that of **abantiare* > French *avancer*.

5. Provençal *trobar*, French *trouver* 'to find'. Meyer-Lübke[5] remarks that the derivation of these words from *turbare* 'to disturb' rests on the undemonstrable assumption that the Latin verb developt the meaning 'to pulsate'. The phonetic anomalies presented by the etymology *trouver*, *trobar* < *turbare* are also considerable, including (aside from the defensible metathesis) the assumption of an irregular stem-vowel in Old French *trueve*, Provençal *trǫba*, which naturally suggest that the etymon had an open *o*, and the difficult assumption of the persistence of *b* in Provençal which seems rather to show that the etymon contained the sound *p*.

As an alternative which has hitherto remained unnoticed, so far as I am aware, I suggest derivation from the Frankish stem *top*, which according to Diez, followed by Körting, gives Spanish *topar*, Italian *intoppare* 'to run across', 'to find'. These words are omitted by Meyer-Lübke, perhaps inadvertently, as he acknowledges the derivation of Spanish *topetar* 'to but' from this stem. The sense-development of *topar*, *intoppare* was evidently 'to but against', 'to run across', 'to find'. The etymology which I propose cannot, therefore, be objected to on semantic grounds.

This etymology assumes the metathesized base **tropare* for French and Provençal, while we have developments of the unmetathesized stem

[3] Op. cit.[3]
[4] Op. cit.[3]
[5] Rom. Gram. 2. 448f.
[6] Op. cit.[3]
[7] Et. Wb. d. rom. Sprachen 660 (1887).

in Spanish and Italian. As analogous to this postulation we may cite the Vulgar Latin base *tresaurus, required to account for French and Catalan reflexes, while the unmetathesized base *tesaurus has to be assumed in the case of the corresponding Provençal, Spanish, and Italian words. So, too, we have Italian *torchio* 'press' beside French *treuil* 'windlass', Catalan *trolh* 'oilpress' < Latin *torculum* beside Vulgar Latin *troculum* 'press'. Likewise, Italian *temperare*, Spanish *templar*, beside French *tremper*, Catalan *trempar*, the Provençal dictionary showing for this word (< Latin *temperare*) both metathesized and unmetathesized forms; It. *tonare, tronare*, French *tonner*, Prov. and Span. *tronar* < *tonare*.

When the Latin termination -*are* was added to the Frankish noun-stem *top, the *p* became *pp* in Italy, remained *p* in Spain, and developt like a Latin intervocalic *p* in French and Provençal. This divergent development was due to borrowing in two different periods. The phonological principle involved has been dealt with systematically by Mackel,[8] who divides all Germanic loanwords in Romance into two strata, an earlier one containing the words that participated in the Romance sound-shifts, and a later one including those that did not. I will quote a few pertinent examples. While Frankish *skrapan* 'to scrape' shows a Frankish intervocalic *p* undevelopt in Old French *escraper*, in French *buer*, Provençal *bugar* < Frankish *būkon* 'to buck clothes' we have a case of the development of Frankish intervocalic *k* in French and Provençal. Again, Frankish *pauta* 'paw' gives Provençal *pauta*, without development, but Old French *poue*, with development thru ð. Mackel[9] expressly states that in the first stratum of loanwords, intervocalic Germanic *p* becomes *v* in French, and cites Old Low Frankish *skapid* > Old French *eschevi* 'lithe'. Meyer-Lübke[10] similarly indicates the accepted derivation of Old French *eschevin*, Provençal *escabin* from a Germanic *skapins* 'alderman'.

In the early stratum of loanwords, according to Mackel,[11] free *ǫ* under the main stress becomes in Old French *uo, ue*, and remains *ǫ* in Provençal. One example given is Germanic *hǒsa* > Old French *huese*, Provençal *ǫsa* 'trousers'.

Spanish *topetar* 'to but into' evidently postulates a Vulgar Latin *topittare*, with the VL suffix -*ittare*, as a suffix -*etar* can hardly be said to have been living in the Old Spanish period.

I believe Spanish *tropezar* 'to stumble' likewise comes from a VL metathesized type *tropittiare*.

---

[8] Die germanischen Elemente in der französischen und provenzalischen Sprache. Französische Studien 6. 1 (1887).
[9] Op. cit. 177.
[10] Op. cit.³
[11] Op. cit. 29.

XIII

SPANISH *ALARIDO*; PORTUGUESE *ATANAR*; SPANISH *CINCHAR*; PORTUGUESE *DEITAR*; SPANISH *DEJAR, PINCHAR*

1. Spanish *alarido* 'howl', 'outcry', 'shout', 'scream'.
Meyer-Lübke[1] has two entries referring to this word. In the first, he quotes an old derivation, also accepted by Diez, from an alleged rare Arabic word *arīr* 'exaltation'; in the second, he follows Baist[2], who doubts the existence of this Arabic word, and posits as the etymon the Koranic formula *le ilāh illa allēh* 'There is no god but God', which, he assumes, developt the meaning 'warcry'. In view of the phonetic and other difficulties involved in these derivations, the etymology of *alarido* may obviously be regarded as unknown.

The word is probably borrowed from Basque *alarao* 'outcry', which seems related to Basque *alara* 'cackle', *alaratu* 'to cackle', beside *alarautu* 'to make an outcry'. *Alarao* 'outcry' beside *alara* 'cackle' seems to parallel morphologically Basque *barau* 'a fast', *barautu* 'to eat vegetables', 'to fast', beside *bara* 'vegetable'; *garau* 'fruit', *garautu* 'to head out', beside *gara* 'summit'; *marrau* 'roar', *marroatu* 'to roar', beside *marra* 'bellow'. Other Basque words apparently showing the same ending *-au*, which is not mentioned by Uhlenbeck[3], are *umau* 'preserved fruit' beside *umo* 'ripe'; *arrlau* 'flagstone' beside *arrol* 'flagstone'; and *zamau* 'table-cloth beside *zamu* 'table-cloth'. Azkue[4] suggests another etymology for *alarao*: < *ala* 'pain' + *arao* 'imprecation'. At any rate, the word seems to be of native Basque origin rather than a borrowing from the Spanish.

Basque *alarao* closely resembled Spanish past participles in *-ado* < *-atum*. The adoption of the Spanish ending *-ido* was evidently determined by the analogy of numerous Spanish words of somewhat similar meaning, which assumed the termination *-ido* instead of *-ado*, such as *sonido, bramido, graznido, ladrido, aullido, silbido*, etc.

2. Portuguese *atanar* 'to tan', with Provençal *tanar*, French *tanner*, to which we may add English *to tan*, is referred by Meyer-Lübke[5] to the

[1] Rom. et. Wb.³
[2] Romanische Forschungen 4.374.
[3] De woordafleidende suffixen van het Baskisch; in Koninklijke Akademie der Wetenschappen, Afdeeling Letterkunde, Nieuwe reeks, Deel vi, no. 3, 1906.
[4] Diccionario vasco-español-francés, 1905.
[5] Op. cit. s.v. tanare.

Reprinted from *Lang*. X (1934), 27-31.

type *tanare* 'to tan', a word which, as was noticed by Diez[6], occurs in the Erfurt glosses, and which Meyer-Lübke declares of unknown origin. Derivation from Old High German *tanna* 'oak', suggested by Frisch[7], was thought possible by Diez[7] and Körting[8]; but in view of the fact that the word *tanna* is not attested as a verb in Germanic, nor in the sense of 'fir' or 'oak' in Romance, the etymology seems improbable.

I propose to derive Portuguese *atanar* from Arabic *aṭana* 'to macerate', 'to prepare (hides)', which for the Portuguese presents no phonetic irregularity whatever, inasmuch as Arabic *'ain* regularly disappears in Spanish and Portuguese, while *ṭa* becomes *t*.[9] The dropping of the initial *a-* in Provençal and French may be attributed to a confusion with the numerous Latin words compounded with *ad-*, such as **accoligere* beside *colligere*, Portuguese *acolher*, *colher*, on account of which the supposed prefix was omitted. A similar dropping of the prefix *a-* < *ad-* is clearly shown in Portuguese *samblar* 'to dovetail' beside French *assembler* 'to assemble' < **assimulare*; and less distinctly, owing to the possibility of derivation from uncompounded etyma, by such forms as Catalan *catar* 'to solicit alms' beside Provençal *acaptar* < **accapitare*; Portuguese *olhar* 'to eye' beside Old Portuguese *aolhar* < **adoculare*; Catalan *rosar* 'to sprinkle' beside Provençal *arosar* < **arrosare*.

3. Spanish *cinchar* 'to gird', *cincho* 'belt'.

The verb is derived by Körting, following essentially Diez, from Vulgar Latin **cīngulare*; but Meyer-Lübke[10] justly observes that the word requires phonetic explanation. Indeed, if Tuttle[11] takes the correct view of the phonology, regarding *ungula* > *uña* as normal, **cīngulare* would give **ciñar*; or if, as Menéndez Pidal[12] boldly states, Romance groups are preserved in Spanish when the first consonant is a nasal liquid or *s*, and the third is *l* or *r*, *cīngulare* would regularly become **cinglar*.

I propose to derive *cinchar* from the type **cīnctulare*, with phonology for the group *nct'l* identical with that establisht for *nc'l*, as in *conchula* >

---

[6] Rom. et. Wb. 683.

[7] See Diez, l. c.

[8] Lat.-rom. Wb., s.v. tanna.

[9] Engelmann, Glossaire des mots espagnols et portugais dérivés de l'arabe, xix, xxiv.

[10] Op. cit.

[11] Modern Language Review 8.484f. This article, essentially anticipating my view of the etymology, was brought to my attention by Mr. Tuttle when I suggested the derivation of *cinchar* from **cīnctulare* before the Linguistic Society. Tuttle derived *cincho* directly from **cīnctulum*, mentioning Italian *cintolo* < **cīnctulum*, and incontrovertibly impugning the view, then held by Menéndez Pidal and Zauner, that *cincho* comes from **cingulum*.

[12] Manual de gramática histórica española[5] 135.

concha. I posit the same phonetic development for **pīnctulare* > *pinchar* and *sanctulum* > *Sancho*, discusst below.

4. Portuguese *deitar* 'to throw', 'to spread out', was derived by Diez[13] from *dejectare* 'to hurl down', a word which he found attested in Aulus Gellius, who quotes it from Mattius. The etymology was taken over without question by Körting[14] and Coelho[15], and would hardly call for reinvestigation if it had not been entirely omitted by Meyer-Lübke[16], perhaps on account of its puzzling phonology. A careful review of the analogous developments seems to prove that the development *dejectare* > *deitar* should be regarded as regular: cf. *lectus* > *leito*; the *j* drops like the *g* in *sagitta* > *saeta*; the first two vowels coalesce as in *sigillare* > *sellar*. To be sure, Port. *rejeitar* < *rejectare* has another syllable, but it is a later or semi-learned formation like *despedir* beside *despir* < **deexpedire*.

Meyer-Lübke[4] gives two conflicting and unsatisfactory derivations of the word. Under his number 4568, he suggests that it may be from the type **jectare* thru its regular reflex *geitar*, the *d* being due to a dissimilation, or to the influence of *deixar* 'to leave'; and under his number 4254, he proposes to derive *deitar* 'to spread out' from *ictus* 'blow', as a verbal compound. The first etymology involves questionable phonetic procedure; and the other amounts to postulating a Vulgar Latin **deictare*, a formation which, unsupported by analogies, seems unacceptable. While the meaning 'to spread out' is an interesting shift of the sense 'to hurl down', it does not appear to indicate a separate etymon.

5. Spanish *dejar*, OS *dexar* 'to let go', 'to abandon', 'to leave', and Portuguese *deixar*, with the same meanings, are commonly derived from *laxare* 'to relax'. However, the transformation of initial *l* into *d*, involved in this etymology, has never been convincingly defended. In connection with a trenchant criticism of the phonetics of this traditional derivation, G. G. Nicholson[17] has proposed to derive the words from the type **decessare*, assumed to have the meanings of *decedere* 'to retire', 'to yield'. He asserts that **decessare* regularly develops into OS *dexar*, taking for granted, without discussion, that Latin *c* was still a velar stop when the second vowel of **decessare* dropt. While analogous words are not numerous, the develop-

---

[13] Op. cit. 161.
[14] Op. cit. s.vv. *dejecto* and *ejecto*.
[15] Diccionario manual etymologico da lingua portugueza, n.d.
[16] Op. cit.
[17] Revista de filología española 19.278–283. Mentioning the formula of Schuchart following Ascoli (*laxare* + *delaxare* = **daxare*) and Meyer-Lübke's notion that the *d* of *dexar* is from *dare*, Nicholson pertinently declares that these conjectures cheapen phonetics.

ment of *amicitatem* > OS *amizdat* indicates that *c* preceding *e* or *i* had become *ts* at the time in question. OS *rezar* (apparently thru **rezdar*) points in the same direction. Inasmuch as the intermediate phonetic type **detsessare*, which seems indicated, would not become *dexar*, but probably **dessar* in OS, Nicholson's etymology appears to be undemonstrated, and, in view of the absence of proof of the survival of *decedere* in Vulgar Latin, improbable.

I propose to derive OS *dexar*, Port. *deixar* from **dejectiare* 'to throw down', which presents no semantic difficulty. In the absence of analogous popular words, the regularity of the development of *cty* into OS *x* cannot be proved. Ford[18] and Hanssen[19] have held that *sty* becomes *x* in *OS*; and since intervocalic *ct* gives *ch* (*factum* > *fecho*), while *ty* after various consonants becomes *ç* (**cuminitiare* > *començar*), it seems likely that *cty* also develops into *x*, rather than into *ç* or *ch*.[20] The other features of the assumed development are clearly regular: according to the rule for analogous words stated by Menéndez Pidal,[21] the pretonic vowel regularly disappears; and Latin *j* or *g* before front vowels regularly drops, as in *sagitta* > *saeta*[22]. The *i* in Port. *deixar* seems analogous to the *i* in Port. *correia* beside Span. *correa*, and may be regarded as regular.

6. Meyer-Lübke[23] assigns Spanish *pinchar* 'to puncture', along with French *pincer* 'to pinch', Italian *pinzare* 'to prick', to an onomatopoetic type **pīnctiare* 'to prick'.

The phonology of the derivation *pinchar* < **pīnctiare* rests on a very weak foundation. Hanssen[24], indeed, affirmed that the phonetic group in question gave *nch* in Spanish; but the only examples alleged are **cinctiare* > *cinchar* and **sanctium* > *Sancho*; and these are erroneous derivations, as is shown above and below. Ford[25] has demonstrated that *ty* following a consonant becomes *ç* in Old Spanish, and Menéndez Pidal[26] recognizes this as the normal development, citing **punctionem* > *puyçon*, **alabantia*

---

[18] Old Spanish Sibilants 120.
[19] Spanische Grammatik 55.
[20] Mr. E. H. Tuttle, in the public discussion of this etymology, suggested that the phonology of **collacteum* > *collaço* invalidates the derivation here presented; compare his treatment of the word *collaço* as a regular popular development in Modern Language Review 8.493f.; but see also Hanssen, Span. Gram. 55, who regards it as irregular. The accented vowel may indicate that it is semilearned; compare **lacte* > *leche*.
[21] Op. cit. 61.
[22] Menéndez Pidal, op. cit. 109f.
[23] Op. cit.
[24] Op. cit. 56.
[25] Op. cit. 39–43.
[26] Op. cit. 122.

> *alabança, criança, assechança*. The rule stated by Hanssen is thus shown to be wrong.

I propose to solve the difficulty by postulating the etymon **pīnctulare* for *pinchar*, with phonology for the group *nct'l* identical with that of *nc'l*, as indicated above.

Further, it is plainly inadmissible to regard these words as onomatopoetic if a Latin source can be found for them; and they can be connected, in both form and meaning, with Latin *pingere* 'to tattoo', 'to embroider', 'to paint'. Diez[27], to be sure, argued that the meaning 'to embroider' does not justify the postulation of the sense 'to prick' for the Vulgar Latin word, but is merely an extension of the meaning 'to paint'. However, the ancient word is shown by its congeners[28] to have had in Indo-European the meaning 'to scratch', 'to cut'. Both Fay[29] and Hirt[30], quoted approvingly by Walde[31], hold that the IE word was used, like its Latin reflex, in the sense of 'to tattoo', hence meant both 'to prick' and 'to paint'. The postulation of Vulgar Latin *pingere*, **pictare* 'to prick', 'to paint', with the derivatives **pīnctiare*, **pīnctulare* assuming only the meaning 'to prick' (whence 'to pinch'), thus seems justified. The Vulgar Latin participle **pīnctus*, already postulated in Körting[32], is easily explained as due to the analogy of *punctus*, itself an irregular classic Latin formation instead of **puctus*, from *pungere* 'to prick'. A further support for the postulation of the etymon **pīnctulare* may be seen in the fact that VL **pictare* 'to paint' certainly assumed the form **pīnctare* in Spain, as is evidenced by the Spanish resultant *pintar* 'to paint'.

7. Spanish *Sancho*, a proper name, < *sanctulum* 'little saint'. See Ford, Old Spanish Readings 284.

[27] Op. cit. 251.
[28] E.g., Sanskrit *piçati* 'to hew out', 'to adorn'; see Walde, Lat. et. Wb.² 583.
[29] See Walde, Lat. et. Wb.² 584.
[30] See Walde, Lat. et. Wb.² 584.
[31] Lat. et. Wb.², s.v. pingere.
[32] Op. cit., s.v. pingere.

XIV

MORE ON PORTUGUESE *DEIXAR*, SPANISH *DEJAR*, SICILIAN *DASSARI*

In *Language* 10.29–30 (1934) I proposed to derive Portuguese *deixar*, Old Spanish *dexar*, Spanish *dejar* 'to leave' from Vulgar Latin **dejectiare*, a suffixt form of *dejectare* 'to throw down.' This attested Latin word, originally noticed by Diez and unfortunately ignored by Meyer-Lübke, regularly became Port, *deitar* 'to throw,' 'to spread out,' as I showed in the same article. However, Tuttle,[1] by adducing Spanish *derezar* < **directiare* and *trazar* < **tractiare*, has apparently demonstrated—since **dejectiare* would have to be assigned to the same chronological stratum—that *cty* cannot give *x* in Old Spanish, thus rendering the etymon **dejectiare* improbable. Nevertheless, Nicholson's methodological denunciation[2] of the Ascoli-Schuchardt formula *laxare* + *delaxare* = **daxare* (reasserted by Tuttle in his article) is still entitled to consideration, although the Australian scholar's derivation of *dejar* from **decessare* is, as I have shown,[3] probably wrong.

I now present a new and, I believe, definitive solution of this old etymological puzzle. *Deixar*, *dexar*, and *dejar* come from Vulgar Latin **dejexare*, a popular variant of *dejectare* 'throw down.' Spanish *dejar* < OS *dexar* < VL **dejexare* is plainly regular, the dropping of the *j* being paralleled by *sigillum* > **sijillu* > *sello* and *sagitta* > **sajitta* > *saeta*. Further, the yodh in Old Portuguese *leixar* 'to leave' < *laxare* 'to release' appears to prove that the yodh in Port. *deixar* < **dejexare* is likewise regular. Even if it were irregular, it might be explained as due to contamination with *deitar* 'to throw' < *dejectare*, where it is regular.

The postulated VL **dejexare* is from a participle **dejexus* taking the place of the attested *dejectus* 'thrown down.' This postulation, which the regular Hispanic resultants seem to make inevitable, is sufficiently supported by the participial pairs mentioned by Sommer:[4] *fixus fictus*, *fluxus fluctus*, *frictus frixus*. To these we may add the pairs adduced by Ulrich:[5]

[1] *Romanic Review*, 26.31–33 (1935).
[2] *Revista de filología española*, 19.278–289.
[3] *Language*, 10.29 (1934).
[4] *Handbuch der lateinischen Laut- und Formenlehre* (1902), 645.
[5] *Zeitschrift der romanischen Philologie*, 4.383. These forms were adduced in support of the etymon **sexicare* suggested by Ulrich to explain Spanish *sesgar* 'to cut obliquely.'

fartus farsus, indultus indulsus, mertus mersus, emulctus emulsus, pultus pulsus, sartus sarsus, scriptus scripsus, tentus tensus, tertus tersus, tortus torsus.

In my former article on this subject, I failed to discuss Sicilian *dassari* 'to leave,' an omission lamented by Tuttle.[6] It is also from **dejexare*, the irregular stem-vowel being due to confusion with *laxare* 'to release,' which became *lassari* 'to leave' in Sicilian.[7] These are various examples of the dropping of VL intervocalic *j* in this territory: *friiri* beside *frijiri, fuiri* beside *fujiri, leiri* < *legere*, etc.[8] While the rules for syncope in Sicilian are not clear, it is obvious that when the *j* dropt, **dejexare* must have become **dexare*. In short, **dexare* (< **dejexare*) + *laxare* = **daxare* > *dassari*.

[6] Article cited (*Rom. Rev.* 26.31–33).
[7] J. W. Ducibella, *The Phonology of the Sicilian Dialects* (1934), pages 473–475, quoting Wentrup and Gregorio.
[8] Ducibella, *op. cit.*, quoting Avolio.

XV

SPANISH *COLUMBRAR* 'TO DESCRY', *VISLUMBRAR* 'TO SEE DIMLY'

Columbrar was derived by Schuchardt[1] from *calīgo* 'darkness', 'dimsightedness.' Meyer-Lübke[2] finds this conjecture dubious because it presupposes an unattested **calumbre* 'shortsightedness'. He might have added that the initial syllable of *columbrar* naturally points to an etymon beginning with *co-*.

The dictionary of the Spanish Academy, followed by Spitzer,[3] has connected *columbrar* with *colluminare* 'to illuminate on all sides,' but neither the Academy nor Spitzer explains the considerable change in meaning. The latter remarks somewhat vaguely: "La différence de nuance ('illuminer *complètement*—'voir *à demi*') ne me semble pas offrir de difficulté." Meyer-Lübke, referring to Spitzer's article, declares the etymology *columbrar* < *colluminare* "begrifflich nicht annehmbar," evidently because the meanings 'to illuminate' and 'to see' are not obviously related. However, I shall revert to the etymon *colluminare*, and endeavor to demonstrate its correctness; first mentioning two other etymologies which have, rightly in my opinion, been rejected by Meyer-Lübke on phonetic grounds.

Menéndez Pidal[4] saw in *columbrar* a derivative of *columna* 'column'; but, as Meyer-Lübke observes, we do not find original classical Latin *mn* becoming *mbr* in other Spanish words. Américo Castro[5] suggests derivation from **columinare* for *culminare*, but Meyer-Lübke, again justly, objects because this presupposes an unexplained change of *-lm-* into *-lum-*. *Columen* for *culmen* occurs regularly in Plautus, but it has a short *u*.

Returning to *colluminare*, we may note that according to the Latin lexicon the phrase *male luminatus*, meaning 'shortsighted,' occurs in the *Metamorphoses* of Apuleius. Hardly more than a shift in voice was, then, necessary to give the word *luminare* the meaning 'to see.' And there is evidence that such a shift did occur; I refer particularly to the analogy of Spanish and Portuguese *vislumbrar* 'to glimpse,' 'to have a glimmer of',

[1] *Zeitschrift. f. rom. Phil.*, XXVII, 614.
[2] *Rom. et. Wb.* (3rd. edition.).
[3] *Revista de Fil. Esp.*, XIV, 243.
[4] *Romania*, XXIX, 344.
[5] *Revista de Fil. Esp.*, XIV, 243 (footnote).

'to see imperfectly at a distance,' derived by Diez,[6] followed by Coelho,[7] from *bis + lumbre* (<*lumine*). Comparing the words *columbrar* 'to see at a distance' and *vislumbrar* 'to see imperfectly at a distance,' it is hard to escape the conviction that they contain the same stem, and that this stem is that of Latin *lumen* or *luminare*. *Deslumbrar* 'to dazzle,' already mentioned by Spitzer, quite obviously has the same stem. Beside *vislumbrar* we have also the noun *vislumbre*, and Catalan *besllum, besllumar*.

The passage from the sense 'to illuminate' to the sense 'to see' is almost exactly identical with the shift of meaning which we find in English *to glare, to glare at* 'to shine', 'to look angrily at', *to glimpse* 'to shine faintly', 'to glance', *to glimmer* 'to shine faintly', 'to look with half-closed eyes.' Again, German *Blick* 'look' is, according to Kluge,[8] from Middle High German *blick* 'gleam', 'lightning', 'look', corresponding to Old High German *blic* 'lightning.' A relation between the meanings 'to shine' and 'to see' is explicitly admitted, in a discussion of the etymology of Latin *considerare*, by Walde,[9] who mentions Lithuanian *žėráti* 'to gleam', a cognate of Old Bulgarian *z'rěti* 'to see.' And lastly, Sanskritists assume the same sense-development for the verb *lokati* 'to see', which according to Macdonell[10] is from *rokati* 'to shine'.

As for the forms, Catalan *besllum* is a regular derivative of **bislūmen*, which was perhaps patterned after a Germanic word like Dutch *twelecht*, English *twilight*. Spanish and Portuguese *vislumbre, vislumbrar* are poorly spelled semi-learned forms. *Columbrar*, like *alumbrar* < **alluminare*, owes its single *l* to the attraction of **lūmĭne* > *lumbre*.

[6] *Rom. et. Wb.*, 497. The rival derivation from *vix luminare*, indicated in the Academy's dictionary, should be rejected because unsupported by analogous formations.
[7] *Diccionario manual etymologico da lingua portuguesa.*
[8] *Et. Wb. der deutschen Sprache* (1899).
[9] *Lat. et. Wb.* (2nd edition.)
[10] *Practical Sanskrit Dictionary.*

XVI

SPANISH *CORRAL, LOCO,* AND *MOZO*

1. CORRAL 'yard,' 'stockyard' was cleverly explained by Diez[1] as a derivative of *corro* 'circle of persons'; *corro* as a verbal noun from *currere* > *correr*. However, Körting[2] having defined *corral* as 'running-place', Meyer-Lübke[3] declares that *corral* 'yard' is unexplained semantically.

To clarify the formation and meaning of *corral*, it is only necessary to observe, firstly, that the suffix *-al* is not attacht to verbs, so that Körting's definition does not exactly fit; and, further, that the formation of *corral* 'large circular space' from *corro* 'circular space' is exactly like that of *ventanal* 'large window' from *ventana* 'window.' In fact, Cejador[4] defines Old Spanish *corral* as meaning *corro grande*.

2. Loco (attested in Juan Ruiz), Portuguese *louco* 'crazy' was associated by Diez[5] with Latin *ulucus* or *alucus* 'owl.' The Latin word is found only once, in Servius on Vergil, Eclogue 8, 55. Altho its phonology is puzzling, it does seem to be the right etymon for Italian *alòcco, alòco,* 'owl', 'clownish man,' *lòcco* 'fool.'

Meyer-Lübke, in the third edition of his dictionary (p. 752, no. 9038 a), while preferring this derivation, questions it on account of the phonetic difficulty occasioned by the Portuguese diphthong, and because of the nonoccurrence of the simple form of *ulucus* 'owl,' with its original meaning, in the Iberian languages. The Spanish derivative *alucón* 'owl' is, to be sure, mentioned by him; but it may be noted that this word, containing the vowel *u* in the second syllable, gives very little support to the etymology in question.

As for other etymologies thus far proposed, I will mention two Arabic derivations recorded by Meyer-Lübke (< *lauke* 'trap' and < Mozarabic *yuka* 'owl'), which are rejected by him on semantic and phonetic grounds respectively; and the derivation from *Glaucus*, the name of a Homeric hero who traded his golden for iron armor, an etymology which Meyer-Lübke declares historically impossible.

I propose to derive *loco* and *louco* from Arabic *lauḳ* 'foolishness,' which

---

[1] *Etymologisches Wörterbuch der romanischen Sprachen.*
[2] *Lateinisch-romanisches Wörterbuch*, 3rd edition.
[3] *Romanisches etymologishes Wörterbuch*, 3rd edition.
[4] *Vocabulario medieval castellano.*
[5] *Op. cit.*, 195.

agrees well with both the Spanish and the Portuguese form, in view of undisputed etymologies showing Spanish and Portuguese intervocalic *c* < Arabic *ḳ*, such as Spanish *recamar* 'to embroider' < raḳama, and Portuguese *falquear* 'to hew square' < *falaḳa*. The meaning occasions no difficulty if we consider the existence of the corresponding feminine adjective *laukā'* 'foolish' (masculine *'alwaḳ*). Indeed, since Romance adjectives are sometimes patterned after feminine etyma (Meyer-Lübke, *Romanische Grammatik*, II, 80 f.), the Hispanic forms may be simply from the Arabic feminine adjective. However, it seems to me more likely that the noun *lauḳ* is the real etymon. An exact semantic parallel supporting this hypothesis is supplied by French *ivrogne* 'drunkard,' 'drunk' < Vulgar Latin *ebrionia* 'drunkenness.'

3. Mozo, OS, *moço* 'youth' is referred by Meyer-Lübke[6] to the type *musteus* 'musty,' 'fresh'; but the phonology of this derivation must be regarded as dubious, inasmuch as Ford[7] and Hanssen[8] believe that *sty* becomes *x* in Old Spanish.

The word is probably from *mucceus* or *muccius* 'sniveling.' *Mucceus* has already been postulated by Diez[9] to account for Italian *moccio* 'snivel,' *moccicone* 'sniveling boy.' Meyer-Lübke[10] also postulates *mucceus* to explain certain dialectic forms, but (implausibly in my opinion) he derives Italian *moccio* directly from *muccus*, explaining the *cci* of *moccio* as due to the plural *mucci*.

While the suffix *-eus* is usually added to designate something made of the thing designated by the primitive noun, it was confused in Vulgar Latin with the suffix *-ius*, properly indicating merely association or connection, not material. Examples of the latter sense may be seen in *gallius* 'many-colored' from *gallus* 'rooster,' and in *furius* 'thievish' from *fur* 'thief'—Vulgar Latin formations listed in Meyer-Lübke's dictionary, and supported by Romance derivatives.

In view of Old Spanish *braço* < *bracchium*, the derivation I propose must be regarded as perfectly regular in phonology.

[6] *Op. cit.*, 3rd ed., 477.
[7] *Old Spanish Sibilants*, 120
[8] *Spanische Grammatik*, 55.
[9] *Op. cit.*, 385.
[10] *Op. cit.*, 469.

XVII

PROVENÇAL *AVALIR*; PORTUGUESE *CANHOS*; ITALIAN *GOFFO*; CATALAN *MIGRARSE*; ITALIAN *MUCCA*; MODERN PROVENÇAL *BOUTAREU, POUTAREL, POUTARO*

Provençal *avalir* 'to disappear', along with Catalan *abalir* 'to destroy', has been derived by Spitzer[1] from Latin *abolēre* 'to abolish'. The conjecture is recorded with a bare question-mark by Meyer-Lübke; and it is indeed very questionable in view of its phonetic irregularity; besides, there is no distinct evidence of the survival of this Classic Latin word in Vulgar Latin.

Avalir is more probably cognate with Old French *avaler* 'to lower', 'to descend', a derivative of *vallum* 'valley'. This etymology involves no phonetic irregularity, but only a different conjugation and a shift of the meaning from that of 'to lower' to those of 'to disappear' and 'to destroy'. In fact these three verbs may be said to be semantically related, if we consider that 'disappearing' is often a result of 'lowering' or sinking out of sight; and 'destroying' may be conceived as a result of 'lowering' taken in the sense of 'throwing down'.

If this etymology is correct, Catalan *abalir*, in view of its single *l*, must be regarded as a Provençal loanword. Its spelling with a *b* may be ascribed to the influence of Latin *abolēre*.

Portuguese *canhos* 'table scraps' was derived by Vianna[2] from *canius 'canine'. Meyer-Lübke declares this semantically difficult; but there seems to be no insuperable difficulty in connecting the meaning 'canine' with the meaning 'table scraps', if we recall the commonness of the custom of giving table scraps to dogs. Meyer-Lübke's tersely stated objection may be due to the fact that the suffix *-ius*, confused in Vulgar Latin with the suffix *-eus*, is usually added to designate something *made of* the thing designated by the primitive noun; so that *canius might have meant originally 'made of the dog', like the Greek τὰ κύνεια 'dog's flesh', instead of 'intended for the dog', 'dog's food'. However, the Vulgar Latin suffix in question occasionally designates merely association or connection, not material; for example in *gallius 'many-colored' from *gallus* 'rooster', and in *furius 'thievish' from *fur* 'thief'; Vulgar Latin formations listed in Meyer-Lübke's dictionary and supported by Romance formations.

[1] See Romanisches Etymologisches Wörterbuch³ 33a.
[2] Apostilos 1.223; Meyer-Lübke, REW³ 1595a.

Italian *goffo* 'loutish' is derived by Diez,[3] followed by Pieri,[4] from Greek κωφόs 'blunt', 'stupid'. But Meyer-Lübke,[5] declaring that this etymon does not explain the *ff*, posits an onomatopoetic *guff* 'clumsy'; he also remarks that Norwegian *guff* 'fat person' and English *goff*, *guff* 'fool', pointed out in this connection by Braune,[6] must for historical reasons be rejected as etyma.

Meyer-Lübke's derivation of the Italian word from the alleged onomatopoetic *guff*, being quite unsupported by argument, is evidently improbable. On the other hand, the phonology of the derivation from κωφόs may be readily defended by quoting Meyer-Lübke himself; for in his Italienische Grammatik 153, he gives five examples of anomalous doubling, the first four of which seem quite analogous; these are *cetto* < *cito*, *brutto* < *brutum*, *mecco* < *moechus*, and *orbacca* < *lauri baca*. In fact, he here states that book-words adopted at a rather late date apparently lengthen the consonant. Italian *mucco* 'mucus' < *mucus* may also be noticed in this connection. These phonological parallels, whatever be their ultimate explanation, seem to me sufficiently numerous to render the etymology *goffo* < κωφόs very probable.

Catalan *migrarse* 'to be bored', 'to languish', has been derived by Spitzer[7] from *migrare* 'to wander'. Meyer-Lübke thinks the derivation improbable, since it involves the assumption that *migrarse* is a book-word. Indeed, the shift of meaning postulated seems very unlikely in the case of a purely learned word.

The Catalan verb is more probably connected with *migranya* 'headache'. While its formation is not normal, it is much like that of Pistojan *rogare* 'to threaten loudly' from *arroganza* 'arrogance'.[8] The process in question is back formation; the analogy of *campanya* : *campar* :: *montanya* : *montar* may also be noted.

The sense 'to be bored' may be connected with that of the etymon proposed, by assuming a semantic shift like that presented in English *to prick* 'to feel a sharp pain', ultimately from *prick* 'a pointed instrument'. The Diccionari de la llengua catalana ab la correspondencia castellana (Barcelona, perhaps 1911) gives for *migrarse* also the meanings 'to shrivel up', 'to become wrinkled' (*aixiquirse*, *arrugarse*), the derivation of which from the primary sense 'to languish' seems to present no difficulty.

[3] Etym. Wtb. d. rom. Spr. 186.
[4] Studi Romanzi 4.168.
[5] REW³ 3907.
[6] Zeitschr. f. rom. Phil. 18.514.
[7] See reference in Meyer-Lübke, REW³ s.v. *migrare*.
[8] Salvioni, ZfrPh. 28.186; Meyer-Lübke, REW³ 55.

Italian *mucca* 'milch cow' is associated by Meyer-Lübke with an alleged onomatopoetic *mukka; but, while the initial sounds *mu-* do suggest the lowing of a cow, the ensuing consonants are hard to explain on this basis, and Meyer-Lübke has not offered any explanation of them.

The word is more probably connected with Vulgar Latin *muccus 'mucus', which gives Italian *mucco* 'nasal mucus'. For the meaning, compare Italian *moccichimo* 'dirty-nosed or whimpering baby', from the same Latin stem.

Modern Provençal *boutareu, poutarel, poutaro*[9] 'mushroom', and French *potiron* 'edible mushroom', 'pumpkin' (also appearing in the phrase *courge potiron* 'pumpkin') are derived by Schuchardt[10] from Arabic *fuṭr* 'toadstool'; but he admits that Arabic *fe* should give French and Provençal *f*, not *p*. His conjecture that the Arabic word, which has Semitic cognates like Aramaic *peṭūrotā*, may have been brought to France by Jewish or Arabic physicians, does not suffice to render the etymology phonetically or historically plausible, notwithstanding Gamillscheg's[11] proposal of the indefensible Syriac cognate *pāṭūrtā*, which he sets down as the etymon of French *potiron*.

I posit the Vulgar Latin type *pottarellu < *pottu 'pot' + the double suffix *-arellu*. Adams[12] gives three adjectival examples of the suffix *-arel*; Meyer-Lübke[13] mentions five French examples of the use of the suffix *-rellu*. As for the sense, the tops of mushrooms may be said to resemble small inverted pots; or the original sense may have been adjectival —'a little (vegetable) for the pot'. The initial consonant of the variant *boutareu* may easily be attributed to the influence of *boutarel* (Old Provençal *botarel*) 'little cask'. The variant *poutaro* is due to the dropping of *-ellu*, the stem left being *pottar-* instead of the ancient *pott-*. The *u* (*ou*) < *ŏ* in all the Provençal forms is regular, as in *portare* > *pourta*, *dormire* > *dourmi*.

French *potiron* represents an augmentative type *pottarone instead of the diminutive *pottarellu. The pretonic vowel of *potiron* may be due to some associative interference, such as that of *petit rond* 'little circle.'

[9] Mistral's spelling.
[10] Z. f. rom. Phil. 28. 156; recorded without dissent by Meyer-Lübke, REW³.
[11] Et. Wb. d. frz. Spr., 1928.
[12] Word-formation in Provençal 402.
[13] Rom. Gram. 2.545.

XVIII

SPANISH *BASTAR, DESPACHAR, RAJAR,* AND *REGUNZAR*

1. **Bastar,** 'to be enough,' along with Italian *bastare,* and Provençal, Catalan and Portuguese *bastar,* is derived by Meyer-Lübke (*REW,* 3d ed.) indirectly from a Vulgar Latin *bastus 'stufft,' which, according to his indication, gave immediately Spanish *basto* 'coarse,' Portuguese *basto* 'compresst,' 'abundant.' The origin of *bastus he declares to be unknown, suggesting that it may be connected with Spanish *bastir* 'equip,' or (following Schuchardt) with Greek *bastazo* 'to bear'; and rejecting *bassitare 'to throw down' (from *bassus*), a constructed etymon suggested by Zauner.

I will point out as the probable source of the Romance verbs the Arabic noun *basṭa* 'extent,' 'capacity,' which is unmistakably reflected in Old Provençal *basta* 'a measure of capacity,' and apparently in Old French *baste* 'basket' (beside the verb *baster* 'to be sufficient'). Corresponding nouns, tho unattested, may have existed in the other Romance languages; or, of course, the Italian verb may be borrowed from the Provençal. The formation of *bastar* from late Vulgar Latin *basta (= Ar. *basṭa*) 'capacity' shows no phonetic or morphological irregularity. As for the semantic shift involved, it may be seen that the meanings in question are related; compare Spanish *llenar* 'to fill,' 'to be full' (said of the moon), formed from *lleno* 'full'; and German *genügen* 'to be sufficient,' from *genug* 'enough.' Spanish *mesurar* 'to measure,' from *mesura* 'measure,' would supply an exact semantic parallel if the verb could assume an intransitive meaning, as English *to measure* can and does. In Spanish *cabida,* 'capacity,' from *caber,* 'to be contained,' and in English *fill,* 'full supply,' from *to fill,* the semantic shift is in the contrary direction.

The adjective *basto* has already been set down by Cejador (*Vocab. med. castellano*) as a postverbal derivative of *bastar*; and this appears to be correct. The primary sense must have been 'abundant,' from which the Spanish sense 'coarse' and the Portuguese meaning 'compresst' are derived.

2. **Despachar, empachar,** 'to dispatch,' 'to hinder.'

In *Language* (VII, 261) I proposed the derivation of these words, along with the Italian cognates, from Vulgar Latin **de-ex-patt-iare,* **im-patt-iare,* hypothetical formations constructed by me, in which the VL stem of **patta,* 'paw,' replaced the Classic Latin stem *ped-* found in Latin *impedire, expedire.*

Reprinted from *HR* III (1935), 340–42.

In a personal letter to me, Professor J. D. M. Ford has indicated his disbelief in the possibility of deriving Spanish *ch* from the VL group *tty*, and has suggested that the Spanish verbs may be Italian loanwords. I had to admit in my article that there are no words definitely proving that *tty* can develop into *ch* in Spanish. On the other hand, the development of the suggested etyma into Italian *dispacciare*, *impacciare* presents no difficulty whatever if we consider that *guttiare gives *gocciare* in Italian. Further, I have been unable to find Old Spanish attestations of the Spanish verbs. It therefore now seems clear that while the Italian verbs are the direct derivatives of the VL verbs postulated by me, the Spanish verbs are, as Ford has suggested, borrowed from the Italian.

3. **Rajar,** Old Spanish **raxar,** 'to split,' is hesitantly referred by Ford (*Old Spanish Sibilants*, 126) to Vulgar Latin *rasclare; that is, *rasiculare, a formation from the past participle of *radere*, 'to scrape,' with a double suffix. Meyer-Lübke (*REW*, 3d ed.) thinks this presents phonetic and semantic difficulty; and he leaves the word unexplained.

The type *rasulare, a legitimate VL formation from *radere—rasus*, has thus far not been suggested in this connection, so far as I know; and I believe it deserves serious consideration. It is true that a *rasulare conceived as a variant of *rasurare* has been proposed as a rival etymon to the group of words which Meyer-Lübke assigns to the etymon *rasclare; but that is another matter (most of the words in the group in question do seem to come from *rasiculare).

I have already pointed out in *Language* (VII, 263) that VL $s + l$ may give OS x. The development seems intrinsically probable, and seems to be disproved by no examples or analogies.

As for the semantic difficulty noted by Meyer-Lübke, it is hard to deny that the meaning 'to scrape' may have changed to that of 'to split,' if we notice that English *to shear* means both 'to clip off' and 'to cut as with a sword.'

4. Old Spanish **regunzar,** 'to narrate,' has been derived by Cornu from *renuntiare*, 'to report'; but Meyer-Lübke (*REW*, p. 596, no. 7213 a) correctly declares the assumed dissimilatory disappearance of the first *n* in the Latin word improbable.

Spitzer (*Revista de Fil. Esp.*, XIV, 254) attempts to connect *regunzar* with Vulgar Latin *rebucinare, 'to toot again,' a formation which García de Diego (*Rev. de Fil. Esp.*, IX, 118) properly constructed to account for Spanish *rebuznar*, 'to bray.' To justify the assumed change of *b* into *g*, Spitzer points out such obviously erratic developments as *regolver*, 'revolver,' and *regoldar*, 'to belch,' alleged on dubious authority to be derived from *revolvitare (Diez, followed by Meyer-Lübke, derives it from a constructed *re-gulare); and to demonstrate that the sense may have changed from that of 'to trumpet' to that of 'to relate,' he cites French slang expressions like *chanter* for *avouer*. Meyer-Lübke (*REW*) is unquestionably right in declaring this etymology even more difficult phonetically than Cornu's, and semantically complicated.

Regunzar is readily derived from Vulgar Latin *recomputiare*, the postulation of which seems comparatively simple when we remember that French *conter*, 'to relate,' is from VL *computare*. The development of the *c* into *g* is quite in line with the consonantal development seen in Provençal *redorta* beside Italian *ritorta*, Old French *revel* from *rebellis*, and various similar forms mentioned by Meyer-Lübke (*Rom. Gram.*, II, 357). The *u* from $\breve{o}$, while irregular, is like the $u < \breve{o}$ in *pulgar*, *lugar*, and *jugar*. The *z* from Vulgar Latin intervocalic *ty* must be regarded as regular, since Ford (*Old Spanish Sibilants*, 76) indicates that VL intervocalic *ty* gives *z*.

XIX

OLD SPANISH *REGUNÇAR* < **RECOMPUTIARE*

In *Hisp. Rev.*, 1939, VII, 75, Spitzer calls attention to the type **recognitiare* proposed by him (*RFE*, XX, 171) as the etymon of OS *regunzar*[1] 'to relate,' and objects to the etymon **recomputiare* proposed by me (*Hisp. Rev.*, III, 341f.) on the ground that "as is well known (*Rom. Gram.*, II, 576) we can accept [*-iare* verbs] only from participles and adjectives...."

It is by no means "well known" that *-iare* verbs were never formed from nouns or verbs. Meyer-Lübke, in *Rom. Gram.*, II, 607 (this is evidently the page to which Spitzer intended to refer) wrote: "Fraglich ist, ob auch von Substantiven und von Verben Bildungen auf *-iare* möglich seien.... ORDINIARE: span. *ordeñar*, port. *ordenhar* nebst dem Subst. aital. *ordigno*, obw. *urden'* Nähzeug scheint von *ordinare* aus erweitert...." In *REW*³ Meyer-Lübke queries, to be sure, the forms **ruminiare*, **recaediare*, but he sets down **ordiniare*, **trebiare* (as a Gallic extension of **trebare*), **excarminiare* (> Venetian *agramiñar*) without indication of doubt, and suggests that **tentiare* may be either from *temptare* or from *tentus*. Further, the Vulgar Latin forms **valliare* > Italian *vagliare* 'to winnow' (: Latin *vallus* 'flail') and **frustiare* > Old French *froissier* 'to shatter' (cf. Dauzat, *Dict. etym. de la langue française*, s.v. *froisser*) show clearly enough that the suffix *-iare* was added to nouns.

It must be admitted that the examples quoted above of *-iare* added to simple noun- or verb-stems are not numerous. However, to defend the type **recomputiare* it is only necessary, since we have in Spanish both *cuento* < *computus* and *contar* < *computare*, to point out some indubitable VL words containing a prepositional prefix + noun + *-iare*. Such words we certainly have in VL **redossiare* > OF *redossier*, **infundiare* > Mallorcan *enfonyar*, **infolliare* > Rum. *înfoia*, **incalciare* > OS *encalzar*, It. *incalciare*, all of which are recorded with unquestionable reflexes in *REW*³.

The morphological objection raised by Spitzer to the etymon **recomputiare* thus appears to be invalid. It may be noticed in this connection that the Johns Hopkins professor has only recently taken the view that

---

[1] I now write the word with *ç*, following a suggestion made by Zauner in a note which he sent me in 1935: "*Regunzar* may come from *recomp(u)tiare* if it had *ç* in OSp (I find *regunçerio* in Berceo); *ty* cannot be supposed as intervocalic as is shown by *contar* (early syncope)." Cejador quotes *reguncerio* 'relato,' 'represión' twice from Berceo, *regunzar* only once. It thus seems that *regunçar* is probably the right spelling.

-*iare* cannot be attached to nouns or verbs in VL, since in *RFE*, 1933, XX, 172, referring to *RFE*, VII, 24, he cited in support of the type *recognitiare the connection of OS *rescrieço* 'cleft (in rock)' with VL *crepitiare, which must represent *crepitare* 'to rattle' + -*iare*.

As for the etymon *recognitiare, it is not quite obvious on the semantic side, the meanings of the related words from *accognitus 'bekannt' (*REW*³) being different in the main, although OF *acointier* and OIt *cointar* do occasionally mean 'to relate.' A more serious disadvantage in *recognitiare, I submit, may reasonably be seen in the fact that it has no closer Hispanic cognates than the Catalan *coindament* and the OS *coinde* (apparently a Provençal loanword) recorded by Meyer-Lübke (*REW*³), beside Spanish *reconocer* 'scrutinize,' 'acknowledge'; whereas *recomputiare has an obvious Hispanic cognate in OS *recontar* 'relate': *le recontava todos sus trabajos* (Baena, p. 60, quoted by Cejador, *Vocabulario medieval castellano*).

XX
FRENCH *POTIRON*

Modern Provençal *boutareu, poutarel, poutaro* 'mushroom', and French *potiron* 'edible mushroom', 'pumpkin' (also appearing in the phrase *courge potiron* 'pumpkin') are derived by Schuchardt[1] from Arabic *fuṭr* 'toadstool'; but he recognizes that Arabic *fā* should give French and Provençal *f*, not *p*; and his conjecture that the Arabic word, which has Semitic cognates like Aramaic *peṭūrotā*, may have been brought to France by Jewish or Arabic physicians, does not suffice to render the etymology phonetically or historically plausible, notwithstanding Gamillscheg's proposal[2] of the indefensible Syriac cognate *pāṭūrtā*, which he sets down as the etymon of French *potiron*.

I posit the Vulgar Latin type *pottarellu > *pottu 'pot' plus the double suffix -*arellu*. Adams[3] gives three adjectival examples of the suffix -*arel*. The occurrence of the suffix in Gallic territory is also indicated by the French examples of the suffix -*rellu* adduced by Meyer-Lübke.[4]

The original sense was doubtless adjectival: 'pertaining to the pot', whence 'vegetable for pottage', 'mushroom', 'pumpkin'.

The *u* (*ou*) *o* in all the Provençal forms is regular, as in *pourta* < *portare*, *dourmi* < *dormire*. The initial consonant of the variant *boutareu* may easily be attributed to the influence of *boutarel* (Old Provençal *botarel*) 'little cask'. The variant *poutaro* is due to the dropping of -*ellu*, the stem left being *pottar*- instead of the ancient *pott*-.

French *potiron* evidently contains the same stem with an augmentative suffix instead of the diminutive suffix used in southern France. In view of the French dialectic forms in -*uron*, the etymological type was perhaps rather *pottūrōne than *pottărōne. The irregular pretonic vowel of *potiron* seems due to some associative interference, such as that of *petit rond* 'little circle'.

[1] Z.f. rom. Phil. 28.156; recorded without dissent by Meyer-Lübke, REW³.
[2] Et. Wtb. d. fr. Spr., 1928.
[3] Word-formation in Provençal 402.
[4] Rom. Gram. 2.545.

Reprinted from *Lang.* XII (1936), 51-52.

XXI

CATALAN *ABALTIR*; ITALIAN *CANSARE*; EXTREMADURAN SPANISH *DESTORGAR*; CATALAN *ENCONAR*; SPANISH *LASCA, REGAZAR*

Catalan *abaltir* 'to put to sleep' has been derived by Brüch[1] from the assumed *t*-preterit of Gallic **adbalo* 'to perish'; but Meyer-Lübke[2] regards this etymology as improbable inasmuch as we do not know that Gallic had a *t*-preterit. Spitzer[3] has suggested the derivation of *abaltir* from **expavitare* 'to scare', a notion which Meyer-Lübke pronounces phonetically and semantically unacceptable.

I believe the Catalan verb is from the Vulgar Latin type **abballitare*, formed from VL *ballare* 'to dance'. The prefix and suffix hardly require justification. The change of conjugation may be due to the analogy of Catalan *condormir* 'to put to sleep'. The semantic shift postulated is: (1) 'to dance', (2) 'to make to dance', (3) 'to rock', (4) 'to rock to sleep', (5) 'to put to sleep'.

Italian *cansare* 'to set aside', 'to avoid' is properly derived by Diez[4] from Latin *campsare* 'to sail by'; but this scholar errs, in my opinion, in separating the Italian verb, on semantic grounds, from Spanish *cansar* 'to tire', and deriving the latter word from *quassare* 'to shake'. Körting[5] derives both the Italian and the Spanish word from *campsare*, suggesting that the original meaning of *cansar* was 'to bend (the limbs)'. The considerations presented below will show that this is essentially correct. Menéndez Pidal (Cantar de mio Cid 532) also derives *cansar* from *campsare*, though without discussing the change of meaning. However, Meyer-Lübke[6], following Diez, declares the notions 'to sail by' and 'to weary' semantically remote, and derives *cansar* from *quassare* without explaining the *n*.

The key to the puzzle is to be found in the Greek lexicon. Latin *campsare* is scantily attested, in Ennius and Priscian; but its connection with Greek *kámptein*, admitted for example by Walde[7], appears never to have been

[1] Biblioteca dell' Archivum Romanicum, 2nd series, 3.27.
[2] Rom. et. Wb., 3rd ed., no. 909, s.v. *ballare*.
[3] BdAR, 2.2.
[4] Et. Wb. der rom. Sprachen 362.
[5] Lat.-rom. Wb., 3rd ed.
[6] REW, 3rd ed., numbers 1562 and 6939.
[7] Lat. et. Wb., 2nd ed., s.v. *campus*.

questioned. The starting-point for the Latin form is the aorist *kámpsai*. The Greek verb means (1) 'to bend', (2) 'to turn (a horse or chariot) round the turning post', 'to double a headland', and (3) 'to bend or bow one down' (this sense attested in Aeschylus and Thucydides). While the meaning of Italian *cansare* 'to avoid' < *campsare* 'to sail by' obviously goes back to the second sense of the Greek word, it seems probable that the Latin etymon also had the third sense, 'to bend or bow one down', from which the meaning of Spanish *cansar* 'to weary' is easily derived. The etymological principle here involved has been set forth in LANGUAGE 5.25–6, where I have pointed out, in a discussion of Spanish *sima* 'abyss' < *sīmus* < Gk. *sīmós*, that meanings unattested in Latin words borrowed from the Greek, but attested in their Greek originals, sometimes best explain the sense-development of their Romance reflexes.

Extremaduran Spanish *destorgar* 'to break oak branches while removing acorns', which is not mentioned by Diez, Körting, or Meyer-Lübke in their dictionaries, may be derived without phonetic difficulty from Vulgar Latin **deextorticare* 'to twist off'. A VL **torticare* 'to twist' (from *torquere*—*tortus*) has already been postulated by Ulrich[8] to account for French *torcher* 'to wipe'. Meyer-Lübke[9], to be sure, views **torticare* as an 'unnecessary' formation, explaining the French verb as a secondary derivative, from French *torche* 'rag' < VL *torca*.

Catalan *enconar* 'to taste', 'to give the first milk to a baby', 'to poison', 'to harm', 'to anger'; *enconado* 'accustomed', 'angered'; Spanish *enconar* 'to inflame', 'to anger'; *encono* 'soreness', 'rancor'. This group was connected by Diez[10] with Latin *melancholia*, and the etymology was recorded without dissent by Meyer-Lübke in the second edition of his dictionary; but it is not even mentioned in the third edition, which records only Spitzer's derivation of the words from Latin *inquinare* 'to befoul'. This connection, however, obviously presents great phonetic difficulty.

I derive the group from Vulgar Latin **inconare* 'to test', the formation and assigned meaning of which appear to be indicated by the Romance forms, considered in connection with Logudorian *konos* 'temptation to vomit', which Meyer-Lübke[11] records as a derivative of Latin *cōnārī*.

Spanish *lasca* 'small, thin piece detacht from a stone', Portuguese *lasca* 'small fragment', evidently connected with Spanish *lascar* 'to slacken (a rope)', Portuguese *lascar* 'to shatter', have been derived by Gröber[12] from

---

[8] ZfromPhil. 9.429.
[9] REW, 3rd ed., s.v. *torques*.
[10] Et. Wb. d. rom. Sprachen 446.
[11] REW, 2nd and 3rd editions.
[12] Archiv f. lat. Lex. u. Gram. 3.310.

Gothic *lasca 'rag'; but this etymology is declared by Meyer-Lübke[13] to be semantically impossible.

The Spanish and Portuguese verbs are from Vulgar Latin *laxicare 'to loosen'; and the noun lasca is a postverbal which originally meant 'a loosening', 'something loosened', whence 'a fragment'.

VL *laxicare has already been postulated by Ulrich[14] to account for French lâcher 'to loose' and its cognates. Meyer-Lübke's rejection of this etymology in favor of Regula's *lascus for laxus[15] seems wrong.

Spanish regazar 'to tuck up', regazo 'lap' are associated by Diez[16] with Basque galzarra 'bosom'. This etymology, presenting obvious phonetic difficulty, is not mentioned by Körting or Meyer-Lübke, who omit the Spanish words.

I derive the Spanish verb from Vulgar Latin *recaptiare 'to catch up', 'to tuck up', the formation of which, as well as the assigned meaning, is definitely supported by Rumanian acăța 'to seize', 'to begin', 'to hang' (< VL *accaptiare). The development of VL c into g after the prefix re- has various parallels, on which I refer to Meyer-Lübke, Rom. Gram. 1.357. The noun regazo evidently meant originally 'tuck', 'folded part (of the dress)'.

[13] REW, 3rd ed.
[14] ZfromPhil. 9.429.
[15] ZfromPhil. 44.651.
[16] Et. Wb. d. rom. Sprachen 482.

XXII

SPANISH *HALAGAR, NESGA, SOCARRAR*

Spanish *halagar*, Old Spanish *falagar* 'to wheedle,' along with Catalan *afalagar*, Portuguese *afagar*, having the same meaning, is referred by Meyer-Lübke[1] to Arabic *ḥalaḳa*, defined as 'glatt machen'; but since this Arabic word, spelled with hha (ḥ), not cha (ḫ), means 'to shave (the head, etc.),' the etymology stated by Meyer-Lübke is evidently erroneous. Lokotsch[2] derives the Romance group from the intensive form of *ḥalaḳa* 'to create'; that is, *ḥallaḳa*, defined as meaning 'schön formen, glatt machen, Lügen erfinden'; but if the etymon contained a double *l*, it would have remained as *ll* in Spanish, as Baist[3] long ago pointed out. Baist himself met this difficulty by assuming that the first stem of *ḥalaḳa*, meaning normally 'to create,' must also have had the sense of the intensive stem, which, he says, was used in Spain meaning 'to beguile.'[4] A more satisfactory starting-point, avoiding both phonetic difficulty and problematic definition, is the third stem of *ḥalaḳa* 'to create'; that is, *ḥālaḳa*, 'to treat (a person) kindly.' The slight semantic shift involved obviously presents no difficulty.

Spanish *nesga* 'gore (in a dress)' has been derived by Regula[5] as a contamination of **sēsecāre* 'to cut apart' with *nexus* 'connection.' The etymology is pronounced doubtful by Meyer-Lübke[6] on the ground that there is no trace of the survival of *nexus* in the Iberian peninsula. *Nesga* is doubtless simply a postverbal derivative of Vulgar Latin **nexicare* 'to connect,' and thus meant originally 'a connecting piece.' Similarly, Spanish *rosca* 'screw-thread,' 'screw and nut' is derived from Vulgar Latin **rosicare* 'to gnaw,' by postverbal formation, as I have demonstrated [*PMLA*, xx, 342 f.]. Meyer-Lübke[7] has recently questioned the latter derivation on the alleged ground that the verb is not found in the Iberian peninsula, in spite of Portuguese *rosegar*, which he mentions along with Italian *rosicare* and Provençal *rozegar*. In view of the phonological and morphological attractiveness of the derivation of *nesga* from **nexicare*,

---

[1] *Rom. et. Wb.*, 3rd ed.
[2] *Et. Wb. der europ. Wörter orientalischen Ursprungs.*
[3] *Rom. Forschungen*, IV, 357.
[4] Baist quotes Pedro de Alcalá as saying that *ḥallaḳa* means *sossacar*.
[5] *Z. R. Ph.*, XLIII, 131.
[6] *Rom. et. Wb.*, 3rd ed.
[7] *Rew*, 3rd ed., s.v. **rosicare*.

I suggest that absence of related popular words from the same stem should not be given undue weight.

Spanish *socarrar* 'to singe' is derived by Diez[8] from Basque *sukaŕtu* 'to burn.' He quotes Larramendi as saying that the first syllable of *sukaŕtu* may be identified with Basque *su* 'fire'; the second syllable with Basque *gaŕ* 'flame' (which he cites in the form *carra*). Since the Basque suffix *-tu* corresponds morphologically with Latin *-are*, the formal relation of *socarrar* to *sukaŕtu* almost amounts to identity, particularly if we notice Spanish *motil* 'farmer's boy' < Basque *mutil*, and Old Portuguese *mogo* 'landmark,' probably from Basque *muga*, both Romance words showing the vowel *o* from Basque *u*. However, Diez evidently regarded the initial syllable of *socarrar* as having an irregular vowel, since he explained it as due to the influence of the Spanish prefix *so-* from Latin *sub-*, seen in the synonym *soflamarse* 'to scorch oneself.'[9] Meyer-Lübke,[10] following Schuchardt,[11] questions the etymology because the simple verb is not found in Spanish. [Since Meyer-Lübke's reference to Schuchardt's note is erroneous,[11] I have been unable, in spite of considerable searching, to find the exact words used by the latter scholar; however, Meyer-Lübke's summary may of course be regarded as correct.]

Here, again, the absence of corroborative Romance words may be merely accidental. It is not hard to find compound derivatives of Latin verbs having no corresponding simple verbs in Spanish; for example, *sospechar* < *suspectare*, OS *sosañar* < *subsannare*. On the semantic side, it is highly significant that *socarrar* means 'to burn' in Old Spanish. Cejador[12] gives two examples of this meaning, and indicates that it is common. The meaning 'to burn lightly,' 'to singe' thus appears to be a modern development due to the semantic influence of the prefix *so-*, which the Spaniard, as Diez suggests, felt in the initial syllable.

[8] *Et. Wb. d.* [see note 3].
[9] Diez gives the form *sollamar*, which I cannot verify.
[10] *Rew*, 3rd ed.
[11] *Rieb*, 6.8.
[12] *Voc. medieval castellano.*

XXIII

SPANISH *CHISTAR, REMATAR, SOLLO, TUSA*

1. Spanish *chistar* 'to utter a sound, or to act as if speaking,' generally used with a negative, has been referred by Menéndez Pidal[1] to *sciscitari* 'to inform oneself'; but this suggestion has been properly rejected by Meyer-Lübke[2] on phonetic grounds.

Modern Spanish has a corresponding substantive *chiste* 'facetious remark'; and Cejador[3] quotes from Berceo Old Spanish *chista*, used in the same sense.

The source of the Spanish words is evidently Basque *txistu* 'to whistle,' the phonetic correspondence amounting almost to identity. The meaning 'to make a sound,' while thus far unattested in OS, must be the original sense. The meaning 'jest' is plainly secondary.

2. Spanish *rematar* 'to complete (a thing),' 'to end the life of (a dying person or animal),' 'to shoot dead,' 'to fasten the last stitch with other stitches or a special knot,' 'to knock down (at auction)' is traditionally analyzed into the prefix *re-* + *matar* 'to kill.' Monlau[4] ascribes this etymology to Cabrera, Diez[5] records it with a question mark, and the Spanish Academy[6] sets it down without discussion. Yet Meyer-Lübke[7] declares this explanation semantically impossible; rejecting, furthermore, Menéndez Pidal's derivation[8] of the word from *ramus* 'branch,' i.e., 'to decorate a thing with branches to show its completion.' Meyer-Lübke thus leaves *rematar* unexplained.

Now, it is not difficult to perceive that the old etymology is correct if we consider some of the secondary meanings of the simple verb *matar*: 'to bevel,' 'to round' (a term used by carpenters), 'to mat (reduce the brilliance of [metal]),' 'to tone down' (in art). The simple verb has thus assumed the sense 'to work over or finish off (in various specific ways).' The prefix *re-* merely adds emphasis as in *realegrarse* 'to rejoice exceedingly,' *repudrir* 'to rot much,' *revolcar* 'to knock down' from *volcar* 'to upset.'

[1] *Romania*, v. 29, p. 345.
[2] *Rom. et. Wb.*, 3rd ed., p. 637.
[3] *Vocabulario medieval castellano*.
[4] *Diccionario etimológico de la lengua castellana* (1881).
[5] *Et. Wb. der rom. Sprachen*, p. 468.
[6] *Diccionario de la lengua española*, 15th ed.
[7] *Rom. et. Wb.*, 3rd ed., p. 582, no. 7035.
[8] *Romania*, v. 29, p. 364.

Reprinted from *HR* VI (1938), 75-76.

The compound *rematar* has thus naturally assumed the meaning 'to finish off well,' 'to complete.'

3. Spanish *sollo* 'sturgeon' (also, secondarily, 'pike') was connected by Diez[9] with Latin *suīllus* 'swinish,' and this etymology is recorded without dissent by Meyer-Lübke,[10] who thinks that Portuguese *solho* 'sturgeon' is borrowed from the Spanish. Nevertheless, the derivation of *sollo* from *suīllus* can readily be seen to be phonetically impossible.

The right etymon is the attested Latin *sŭcŭlus* 'little boar,' which regularly becomes Port. *solho*. The Spanish word is borrowed from the Portuguese.

4. Spanish *tusa* means 'corncob' in South America and Cuba; 'spathe of the ear of corn' in Central America and Cuba; 'cigarette made of a cornstalk leaf' in America and Andalusia; 'corn-tassel' and 'horse's mane' in Chile. Its geographical distribution, as well as its association with an American plant, might seem to indicate that it is of American Indian origin; but so far as I am aware, no etymology of the word has ever been suggested in any book or printed article. Dr. J. A. Mason of the Museum of the University of Pennsylvania, to whom I referred the question of possible American Indian origin for the word, is of the opinion that, if American at all, it would most likely be of Arawak (Tainan) origin. He has looked hastily through a few likely sources of information on the subject, such as Marxuach's *El lenguaje castellano en Puerto Rico*, Loven's *Origins of the Tainan Culture, West Indies*, and Koch-Grünberg's *Arawak-Sprachen* without finding any definite indication that *tusa* is of this origin.

I connect *tusa* with Spanish *atusar* 'to trim,' appearing in Argentine Spanish as *tusar* 'to shear,' and derived from Vulgar Latin **tūsare* (for **tonsare*) 'to shear.' It is possible to derive the various meanings of the noun from the fundamental notions of 'something shorn (like the body of a sheep)' and 'something resembling fleece.' Thus 'corncob' and 'corntassel' present different aspects of 'shearing.' 'Spathe' is an extension of 'cob,' and 'cigarette' is from 'spathe' or 'corn-tassel.' Likewise 'horse's mane' is an extension of the meaning 'corn-tassel.'

[9] *Et. Wb. der rom. Sprachen*, p. 488.
[10] *Rom. et. Wb.*, 3rd ed., p. 637.

XXIV

STILL MORE ON *CHISTAR, DEJAR, REGUNZAR*

Chistar 'to utter a sound' with the related substantive *chiste* 'facetious remark', OS. *chista* 'jest' has been connected by me[1] with Basque *txistu* 'whistle'. Spitzer[2] declares the Spanish and Basque words are "elementarverwandt" as "Schallwörter". Without further demonstration than this surmise, it seems to me unlikely that the Spanish word was originally onomatopoetic. The Basque vocabulary at hand[3] does give the exclamation *txist* along with the verb *txist*, with the definitions *chistar, chist!* But both verb and exclamation may have been borrowed from the Basque by the Spanish. The semantic data point in this direction: the Basque definition 'saliva' beside that of 'whistle' is clearly more primitive than the Spanish meanings 'to mutter', 'a joke'.

Dejar. Félix Lecoy[4] says in regard to my derivation[5] of OS. *dexar* from VL. **dejexare:* "On est toujours inquiété de voir invoqué le cas de esp. *sello* < *sigillare* pour rendre compte de la chute du *j* intervocalique. La forme ancienne est régulièrement *seello:* il reste donc à expliquer pourquoi on ne trouve jamais **deexar.*" The difficulty here suggested is instantly solved by consideration of the rule stated by Menéndez Pidal[6] concerning the pretonic internal vowel: "En romance se generalizó la pérdida de la protónica a todas las palabras entre cualesquiera consonantes: *piperata pebrada, iterare edrar, catenatu candado* ..." In *sigillu* > OS. *seello* we have no pretonic *internal* vowel that should have dropt, so the word is not analogous at this point, altho it was properly cited by me to show that the dropping of the *j* in **dejexare* is regular.

Regunzar. Spitzer[7] now admits that the type **recomputiare* may have been formed in VL.: *re* + *computu* + *iare*. Eager to clear himself of the charge of inconsistency, he rashly asserts that *crepitus* in **re-crepitiare* is a participle, altho there is no participle *crepitus* attested before the 13th century, according to the material available in the *Thesaurus Linguae Latinae* and Du Cange. If **re-crepitiare* is not from *crepitare* it is from the attested noun *crepitus*, a connection Spitzer cannot reasonably deny,

---

[1] *Hisp. Rev.*, 1938, VI, 75.
[2] *Lang.*, 1938, XIV, 206.
[3] Lopez Mendizabal'daŕ Ixaka: *Euzkel-Erdel-Iztegia*, 1916.
[4] *Romania*, 1939, XLV, 423.
[5] *Lang.* 1935, X, 29 f.
[6] *Manual de gram. hist. esp.* (5th ed.), 61, §24, 1.
[7] *Hisp. Rev.*, 1941, IX, 347f.

Previously unpublished.

having admitted that *-iare* verbs were formed from nouns. His association of Sp. *ordeñar* 'to milk'—usually and, I believe, properly connected with VL. **ordiniare*—with **ordinium* 'tool' (*REW*, 3rd ed.) is semantically puzzling, since there is no indication in *REW* that the term **ordinium* included utensils. As for the loss of the "etymological link" between OS. *recontar* and *regunzar*, I find a parallel in the OE. *rebondre* beside *repondre* cited by Meyer-Lübke in *Rom. Gram.* I.357. I am also reminded of the current popular form of English *resource* [*risors*], *i.e.* [*rizors*], the latter a mispronunciation often heard over the radio, in which the compound nature of the word is forgotten.

Reverting to the phonology of OS. *regunzar*, if that is the right way to spell the word, it does not appear that syncope had to occur simultaneously in *computare* > *contar* and **recomputiare* > *regunzar*. Hanssen[8] thinks that syncope in Spanish is more recent than the voicing of the intervocalic tenues, instancing **adcapitare* > *acabdar*.

Summing up, the type **recomputiare* still seems to me a more likely etymon for the OS. word than Spitzer's **recognitiare*. It may be recalled that Meyer-Lübke in *Rom. Gram.* I.357 derived *regunzar* from **recomptiare*; but **comptiare* meant 'prepare' ('herrichten'—*REW*), and the semantic gap indicated is hard to bridge.

[8] *Span. Gram.*, 56 f.

XXV

SPANISH *QUEJARSE* 'COMPLAIN'; OLD SPANISH *QUEXAR* 'CONSTRAIN'

Jud's derivation of *quejar* from the type **questiare*, supposedly due to a cross between *quaerere* and *queror*,[1] has been supported by Mack Singleton[2] and opposed by Lawrence Poston, Jr.,[3] whose phonetic objections are controverted by Castro.[4] Castro holds that while the type **questiare* probably did develop the reflex **queçar*, which has not been preserved, the resultant *quexar* should not be regarded as violating phonetic law, since "phonetic tendencies were far from being absolute." I find the Jud-Singleton-Castro theory objectionable first because it is, after all, hazardous from the point of view of phonology, and secondly because the meaning of *quaerere*, 'seek,' is not clearly reflected in any of the numerous examples of OS. *quexar*, *quexado*, etc., which Singleton quotes.[5]

Spitzer,[6] in a four-page article which is not mentioned by any of the above-named scholars, remarking that OS. *quexar* meant '*contraindre, mettre dans une situation de contrainte*' and '*estimular, impeler*,' proposes as the etymon **quassiare*, which is defined in *REW* (3rd ed.) as 'zerbrechen.' Spitzer posits the phonetic series "**quassiare > *quaissar > quejar* d'après la loi de Millardet," and thinks the semantic series 'blesser, fatiguer, éreinter' > 'insister, contraindre, affliger' satisfactory. It is not easy to challenge categorically any single one of the factors constituting this etymological theory—and this may explain why Castro has not attempted to refute it, since it is hard to imagine that he has not read it—yet Spitzer's conclusion remains quite dubious because the "loi de Millardet" is not definitely established, and the assumed semantic shift from 'break up' to 'constrain,' while conceivable, is not sufficiently supported by analogies to seem plausible.

It is thus certainly fair to affirm that the etymology of Sp. *quejarse* remains obscure. In the interest of clearness it may be pointed out that Spitzer's assumption that the etymon of OS. *quexar* meant 'to be in a state of constraint'[7] should obviously be corrected, not only to agree with his

[1] *Homenaje a Menéndez Pidal*, II, 25.
[2] *Hispanic Review*, 1938, VI, 206-210.
[3] *Hispanic Review*, 1939, VII, 75.
[4] *Hispanic Review*, 1939, VII, 169.
[5] Article cited, *HR*, VI, 210.
[6] *Revista de filología española*, 1937, XXIV, 30-33.
[7] Article cited, *RFE*, XXIV, 32: "j'admets comme sens originaire celui de 'estar en aprieto'..."

own definitions quoted above, but also in view of the semantic evidence compiled by Singleton, who says:[8] "It will be observed that *quexar* is used (1) as transitive and (2) as reflexive-reciprocal. No cases of purely intransitive use have been observed." The numerous definitions of OS. *quexar* suggested by Singleton, including 'press someone to do a thing,' 'prevail upon,' 'trouble,' 'harass,' 'afflict,' 'overcome,' 'coax,' 'prod,' 'incite,' 'compel,' are readily connected with the sense of 'constrain'; and this meaning may be found in VL **coaxare*, which I assume to have existed as a variant of Latin *coactare*, the latter word being attested twice in Lucretius with the meaning of 'constrain.'

We may therefore regard the old etymology *quexar* < *coaxare* as formally correct, but the etymon must be defined as meaning 'constrain' instead of 'croak.'

The phonology of the derivation of *quexar* from *coaxare* 'croak' is, to be sure, disputed by Nicholson,[9] who thinks that *coaxare* should have given **cuejar*. However, this contention is contradicted by Tuttle,[10] whose citation of the parallel development of *hac* + *eccum ille* > *aquel*, not **acuel*, seems quite pertinent, although Nicholson in his rejoinder[11] asserts that "*aquel* is merely an example of the elision of a final vowel...." In view of the semantic attractiveness of the etymology **coaxare* (= *coactare*) > *quexar* > *quejar(se)*, which I now propose, it seems to me that Nicholson's view of the phonology involved, since it must assuredly be regarded as supported by very little evidence, should be rejected.

[8] Article cited, *HR*, VI, 206.
[9] *Hispanic Review*, 1939, VII, 74f.
[10] *Hispanic Review*, 1937, V, 349.
[11] Article cited, *HR*, VII, 75.

XXVI

LYONESE *TONA*; SPANISH *ESPITA*; PORTUGUESE *RILHAR*

1. Meyer-Lübke's postulation of a pre-Roman **tauna* (REW³ §8601b) to account for Lyonese *tona*, Forésian *touna*, Southern French and Waldensian *tauna* 'wasp, bee, bumblebee', is plainly erroneous, since all the forms, notwithstanding Meyer-Lübke's explicit assertion to the contrary, can be readily referred to Latin *tabānus* 'gadfly' (REW³ §8507). Meyer-Lübke's objection is based solely on the stress and gender of the Romance words; but the shift of stress to the first syllable of *tabānus* appears also in Sp. *tábano*, the change of gender also in Sicilian *tavana*, and both these words are correctly listed by Meyer-Lübke among the reflexes of *tabānus*. The disappearance of the second vowel in **tabana* (> *tauna, touna, tona*) may be regarded as regular, tho precisely analogous words with *a* in the penult are rare. Grandgent (Provençal Phonology 30, §48) says: 'The unaccented penult vowel that had not already fallen disappeared, in most cases, in the transition from Latin to Provençal.' The examples given include *cǫlp* < *cŏlăphum* beside *cǫlbe* < **colebe* < *colaphum*.

2. The hesitance with which Meyer-Lübke (REW³ §8162) refers Sp. *espita, espitar* 'tap' to **pipa* is fully justified, the indicated phonology being quite wild. The Spanish words appear to contain the same stem as Sp. *espiche* 'meat spit, sharp-pointed weapon' (not mentioned in REW³), and to be derived from the Germanic stem given in two forms in §8163: Goth. *spiuts* 'spit' (giving Sp. *espeto* along with Neapolitan *spitę*, Bergamascan *spet spit*, Logudorian *ispidu*; note the varying stem-vowel) and Frankish *speut* (giving Fr. *épieu* 'boar spear', also Lower Engadinian *spiout* 'wooden peg'). The sense of *espita(r)* may, then, be supposed to have been successively 'spit (pointed implement)', 'to spit (impale)', 'to tap (pierce)', 'a tap (faucet)'.

3. The derivation of Ptg. *rilhar* 'gnaw' from a postulated VL **rodiculare* (Gröber, ALLG 5.239) is rightly rejected by Meyer-Lübke (REW³ §7358), who sets the word down as a derivative of *rōdere* 'gnaw', following Bugge (Romania 4.368), although this obviously presents great phonetic difficulty. Coelho (Dicc. etym. de la lingua portugueza) suggests connection with the stem of Ptg. *rego* 'furrow', a postverbal derivative of Lat. *rĭgāre* 'to water'. A VL **rigulare* 'to furrow' might perhaps form a defensible phonetic base for *rilhar*, but it is not obvious that the meaning 'gnaw' can be developt

out of the meaning 'to furrow', altho a certain resemblance between the two may be admitted.

I am inclined to derive *rilhar* instead from a VL **rĭctulare*, a diminutive of Lat. *ringārī* 'snarl', ppl. *rictus*. A very close parallel to the assumed semantic shift is to be seen in Eng. *gnash* 'grind or strike the teeth together' > 'bite with grinding teeth'. The phonetic development of *rĭctulare* to Ptg. *rilhar*, while not simple, seems regular: **rĭctulare* > **rĭjtulare* > **ritlare* > **riclare* > *rilhar*. 'Lat. *ct* > Port. *įt*: *factum* > *feito* .... The *į of įt* ... contracted with a preceding *į* ... *dictum* > *dito*' (Williams, From Latin to Portuguese 84 f.).

The postulation of *į* instead of *i̯* (> *ę*) in VL **rĭctulare* (which may not be necessary: see below) can be justified by pointing out such VL analoga as **dictu* > Ptg. *dito*, and more particularly **cĭnctu* > *cinto*, **tĭncta* > *tinta*, **pĭnctare* > *pintar*. Here the closeness of the vowel cannot reasonably be referred to a later period, and so Menéndez Pidal (Manual de gramática histórica española⁵ 262), explaining the corresponding Spanish developments, writes *tinto* TĪNCTU *cinto* CĪNCTU to indicate the VL forms **tĭnctu*, **cĭnctu*. I cannot find an analogous case of syncope of -*ct*- + -*l*-, but on the other hand there appear to be no analogous forms suggesting that **rictulare* would have become trisyllabic in Portuguese.

After I had proposed this derivation at the 1941 summer meeting of the Linguistic Society, Professor U. T. Holmes Jr. mentioned OPtg. *relhar* 'gnaw' (which seems to obviate the necessity of postulating a close vowel in the first syllable of **rictulare*) and proposed another etymon for Ptg. *rilhar*. Lat. *religāre* 'bind back', an agricultural term attested in Catullus and Palladius, takes on the meaning 'loosen'. The meaning 'gnaw' may have develop from the sense 'loosen with the teeth'. Grandgent (Vulgar Latin 112, §263) says: 'Intervocalic *g* before the accent fell in many words in all or a part of the Empire, and apparently remained—perhaps under learned or other analogical influence—in others ....' The examples given include **liāmen* beside *ligāre*. The latter word actually appears as *liar* in both Portuguese and Spanish, and this is set down as a regular development by both Menéndez Pidal (Gram. hist.⁵ 108) and Meyer-Lübke (Rom. Gram. 1.373). The development *religāre* > **reliāre* > OPtg. *relhar* thus seems quite possible, even regular.

XXVII

PORTUGUESE *BOROA, ESPIRRAR, FECHAR, PASPALHO, ROSNAR*

1. *Esbroar* 'reduce to dust,' 'destroy' is connected with Port. *boroa, broa* 'maize bread,' which is listed in the REW as a derivative of Gothic *brauþ* 'millet bread.' For the shift in meaning from 'bread' to 'reduce to dust' consider English 'crumb' 'to crumb' 'to crumble.' The Gothic etymon seems to have been overlookt by Gamillscheg in his *Historia lingüística de los visigodos*[1] altho its phonology appears to be clear: $au > o$ as regularly in VL words[2]; an analogical *a* was added to Latinize the loanword; the now intervocalic consonant was regularly[3] voiced; then like intervocalic Latin d[4], the thorn fell in Port.

2. Port. *espirrar* 'to reject', 'throw out' also (intrans.) 'burst out' 'to sneeze', 'to jump' must be from *expīrare* 'blow out'. Coelho[5] derived *espirrar* from *spīrare* but Meyer-Lübke has omitted the word in REW[2,3]. The meaning 'to jump' is evidently secondary. The irregular *rr* is perhaps due to the analogy of *escarrar* 'expectorate' or *esmirrar* 'dry out' verbs similar in sense and in sound respectively.

3. Port. *fechar* means primarily according to the *Pequeno diciondrio brasileiro* (1942) 'to shut unite or join; to lock; to fit together ...' Meyer-Lübke[6] rejecting on phonological grounds Diez's derivation of the word from Latin *factum* has set down *fechar* as a contamination of *pessulum* 'bolt' with an alleged Port. *fermar*[7] 'to shut' which I cannot find in dictionaries. The derivation of *fechar* from *fistulare* proposed by Spitzer[8] is declared by M.-L. to be less probable on the ground that *pechar* occurs beside *fechar*.

I am surprised to find that derivation of *fechar* from VL *fixare* 'to fix' has apparently never been proposed, altho Coelho, in recording Diez's erroneous etymology, has exprest the opinion that *fixare* may have influ-

---

[1] *Revista de filología esp.* XIX *(1932)* 117–150, 229–260.
[2] Williams, *From Latin to Portuguese*, §33.4.
[3] Gamillscheg, *op. cit.*, 255.
[4] Williams, *op. cit.*, §74.1.
[5] *Diccionario etymologico da lingua portugueza.*
[6] In *REW* No. 6441.
[7] Possibly a misprint since the second edition has *firmar*.
[8] *Archiv f. d. Studium d. neueren Sprachen*, 127.159 f.

Reprinted from PMLA LXI (1946), 584–5.

enced the development of the meaning of the Port. word. Semantically *fixare* 'to fix' > *fechar* 'to shut, lock' is easy. As for the phonology, intervocalic $x > \int$ or *ss* according to Williams[9]. If we can posit an open instead of a close *i* in the etymon *fixare*, the derivation is absolutely regular. But can we do this? In view of Italian *fissare* 'to fix', 'to stare at' Provençal *fissar* 'to prick' it is clear that the VL vowel was close in Italian and Provençal territory. However, I suggest that the stem vowel of *fīxi* (from the infinitive *fīgere*) may have been opened in Portugal by the influence of various other VI. verbs having an open stem-vowel, particularly the similar-sounding *fingere fĭnxi* supported by such forms as *cingere cĭnxi*, *pingere pĭnxi*, *stringere strĭnxi*, etc.

4. Port. *paspalho* 'stupid, useless person' (*pessoa estupida, inutil*— Coelho) must be the same as Galician *paspallas* 'quail', listed in $REW^{2,3}$ as a derivative of an attested *quarquara* 'quail'. For the sense cf. Italian *tordo* 'thrush', 'stupid person'. While the phonology of the derivation of the Galician word is obscure the connection of the Port. with the Galician word seems clear.

5. Port. *rosnar* 'to snarl' has apparently not yet been etymologized. I propose to derive it from VL *rosinare a verb based on *rodere* 'gnaw' with the past participle *rōsus*. The suffix *-inare* is not very common, but Meyer-Lübke[10] gives VL as well as Classic Latin examples, e.g. VL (attested) *scarpinare* 'to scrape' > Rumanian *scărpina* 'to scratch'. The shift of meaning from 'gnaw' to 'snarl' seems justified in view of the opposite shift from 'snarl' to 'gnaw' which I have pointed out[11] in attempting to connect Port. *rilhar* 'gnaw' with VL **rictulare : rictus : ringi*:[12]

[9] *Die Gegenstandskulturen Sanabrias und seiner Nachbargemeinden*, 76.
[10] Williams, *op. cit.*, §92.9, p. 87.
[11] *Rom. Gram.* II, §585, p. 611.
[12] *Lang.* xviii 39. Cf. Spitzer, *Hisp. Rev.* X, 344, who accepts the semantic shift 'snarl' > 'gnaw'; questions the form *ringari* erroneously written by me for ClL *ringi*; questions the alleged Old Port. *relhar* quoted by me in reporting Prof. Holmes's theory deriving Port. *rilhar* from Lat. *religare*; and prefers to derive Port. *rilhar* from the already posited *ringulare 'snarl'. The Johns Hopkins professor here predicts that etymologists will soon be limiting their etymological bases to the types already recorded in REW^3. Cf. *Rev. de fil. esp.* 13.116, where Spitzer attempted to derive Sp. *sesgar* 'to cut across' from *sessicare 'to set', instead of the *sesecare proposed by me and adopted in REW^3. I now recognize that Ulrich's etymon *sexicare (:*sexus for *sectus* 'cut') is more probably correct, in view of Hispanic participles in *-x-* for *-ct-*: *dejexare > Sp. *dejar*, *coaxare > Sp. *quejar* (*Hisp. Rev.* VI, 351; IX, 309 ff.), as well as Lat. *fixus fictus, fluxus fluxus, frixus frictus*, etc. (*Hisp. Rev.* VI, 351). *Sexicare was first proposed in *Z. f. rom. Phil.*, IV, 383. [See Williams, *Fr. Lat. to Port.* §41, 3 A, in answer to Spitzer on *relhar > *rilhar*.]

XXVIII

MORE ON κάμπτειν > SPANISH *CANSAR* AND ON GREEK ETYMA IN ROMANCE

Spitzer[1] approves the derivation, advocated by me,[2] of Spanish *cansar* 'to make tired' from Greek κάμπτειν thru Latin *campsare* 'to sail by, to double';[3] but he explicitly rejects the principle laid down by me according to which 'meanings unattested in Latin words borrowed from the Greek, but attested in their Greek originals, sometimes best explain the sense-development of their Romance reflexes.'[4] He tries to explain the apparent change of meaning 'sail by' > 'tire' by positing the semantic series 'sail by', 'deviate' > 'cease', 'fail' > 'get tired'; but the 13th-century Spanish phrases *Non canses de faser oracion* and *Non cansaron*, which he cites in attestation of the intermediate meanings, may have merely the meaning 'to tire'. Without more evidence than the phrase *campsare de via* 'deviate from the way' which he cites from the Peregrinatio, the difficult semantic series proposed must be regarded as unproved and improbable.

On the other hand, why not admit that the Greek-Latin etymon, scantily attested in Latin, had in Latin the meaning 'to bend or bow down', attested in Greek, whence 'to tire' in Spanish? I long ago pointed out[4] that the etymon *platýs*[5] is attested in Latin only in the sense 'broad', while the sense 'flat' appearing in Romance is attested in Greek. If we recall that the Greek and Latin languages were in contact for centuries, it becomes obvious that quite a few Greek loanwords must have been current in Roman speech without all their meanings being recorded in Latin. And I have further proof that this was the case, in the shape of other Greek words appearing in Latin and coming down into Romance with meanings that are attested in Greek but not indicated in Lewis and Short's (Harpers') Latin Dictionary (1891). They are these: (1) ἀγκών 'elbow, bend of a river' : Lat. *ancōn* 'arm of a workman's square' and five other technical meanings : Sp. *ancón* 'small bay'. (2) κέντρον 'any sharp point, sting, center' : Lat. *centrum* 'center, kernel' : Dalmatian *kentra* 'thorn'; Roman *čentrina* 'small

---

[1] *Lang.* 14.205–6.

[2] *Lang.* 13.18.

[3] Definitions from Lewis and Short's New Latin Dictionary, 1891.

[4] *Lang.* 5.25–6.

[5] Given as *plattus* by Meyer-Lübke, REW³, where an asterisk should be added to show that this spelling is unattested, as is done by Dauzat in his Dictionnaire étymologique de la langue française, under *plat*.

Reprinted from *Lang.* XIX (1943), 154–56.

nail'.[6] (3) κλίμα 'slope, clime' : Lat. *clima* 'clime, region' : Abruzzan *klimę* 'incline, inclination'.[7] (4) φάλαγξ 'line of battle, phalanx, camp, log, venomous spider' : Lat. *phalanx* 'band of soldiers, Macedonian phalanx, order of battle of the Gauls and Germans' : It. *palanca* 'stake, palisade'; Sicil. *falanga* 'wooden bridge';[8] Rum. *păringă* 'stake'; Sp. *palanca* 'lever'; and various other Romance reflexes of the meaning 'log', not attested in Latin. (5) σκάφη 'trough, tub, basin or bowl, light boat' : Lat. *scapha* 'light boat' : OFr. *eschafe* 'shell, shellfish';[9] Neapolitan *feyę* 'tub'; Tuscan *scanfarda* 'soup-dish'. (6) σήψ 'serpent whose bite causes putrefaction, putrefying sore, kind of lizard, an insect' : Lat. *seps* 'venomous serpent, woodlouse (?)' : OIt. *sepa* 'small lizard'. (7) σιμός 'hollow, concave, bent upwards, snub-nosed' : Lat. *sīmus* 'snub-nosed' : Sp. *simado* 'hollow', *sima* 'abyss'.[10] (8) στρόμβος 'top, whirlwind, snail' : Lat. *strombus* 'spiral snail' : Istrian *strombo* 'top, pteropod'.[11] (9) τῦφος 'smoke, vapor, conceit' : Lat. *tȳphus* 'pride' : Venetian *tufo* 'vapor'; Cat. *tuf*, Sp. *tufo* 'vapor'; Port. *tufo* 'bubble'.

These examples are surely enough to demonstrate the unwisdom of advocating, as Spitzer does, that in dealing with Greek-Latin etyma we eliminate from our consideration all meanings attested in Greek but not in Latin. Furthermore, it is a pertinent indication that I am here on the right track, and a significant proof of the usefulness of the Greek lexicon in Romance etymology, that about 156 of the Greek etyma in REW³ do not appear at all in Lewis and Short's Latin Dictionary. These are the following, in Meyer-Lübke's transliteration and with a few bracketed glosses of my own: *acastus, acathartos, acula, aegypius, agonos, ambon, ananke, angurium, antisicon, arniskos, atherīne, bikos, bolĭdium, bombyla, boops* [-]*ōpe, boter, bothros, brochis, brōma, brothacus, brŭncus* [I cannot verify this], *cacemphaton, calandra, calāre, calópoios, camba, cara, cardialgia, caryóphyllum, cascāre* [i.e. *chascāre*—χάσκω], *catabŏla, cĕphălus, ceramída, characium* [i.e. χαράκιον], *chēlone, ciccybos, cistus, colla, cŏlŭmbāre, cormus, coscinon, cottĭzāre, cŏtȳlos, cremaster, dēma, dŏlĭchos, empheuein, enydris, ĕrĕbĭnthos, escharium, exartia, fakelos, gadus, gastra, genea, hagios ho theos,*

---

[6] 'Stachel', REW³, number 1815.
[7] 'Neigung', REW³.
[8] 'Holzsteg', REW³, number 6455.
[9] 'Schale, Muschel', REW³.
[10] This etymology of Baist's (ZPRh. 5.563) was rejected by Meyer-Lübke in REW², number 7931, defended by me (*Lang*. 5.25–6), and then accepted by Meyer-Lübke in REW³ with a reference to my article; but Spitzer questions it in *Lang*. 14.206, referring to his fantastically irregular derivation of Sp. *sima* from *sedīmen*, the unreasonableness of which I had pointed out in *Lang*. 5.25.
[11] So REW³, where there is also indicated an Italian *strombo* 'top', which I cannot verify.

hármala, hěctĭcus, hexámetus, himantis, *kamatkon, kamax, kampe, katogeion, kele, keration, kobalos, kophos [etymon rejected by M.-L., but cf. Rice, LANG. 11.239], kótylos, krataegus, kynanche, kyrie eleison, laccanāre, lacchannizesthai, laccus, lambda, limēros [sic, = λīμηρός, Sard. lĭmaru], mactra, makaria, makella, mandrakion, maschale, mesītes, mik(k)ós, momos [etymon questioned by M.-L.], mormo -ous, mystax, nykteris, orax -āce, ŏstrăcum, oxyacanthus, pachys, pagé [read pagē = πάγη], pagium [should apparently carry an asterisk], paidion [doubtful, cf. Rice, LANG. 9.309 f.], panagron, *pandofilo, pantophellos, para, parakōne, pardālus, patassāre, pathēma, peiria, peiron [I find πεῖρος -ους 'spigot' attested in a Mod. Gk. lexicon], pelos, petaknon, phalkis, phantasiāre, phleum, phosphorus, phykis, pitharion, plagius, plema, plōma, plōte, protocollum, prumnon, ptochos, putĭna, rhizikon, riphe, romacus, runcus [= ῥύγχος], rykane, salamandra, sandalon, sardon -one, sauros, scaphus, schema, sēma, skala, skyros, spanos, stŏlĭum, stratiōtes, sykoton, symptoma, tēgănum, tellīne, teuthis, themonia, theophania, thia, thius, thymallus, thymiama, trema, trepein, trĭgle, trĭphyllon, tropaea, trophe, trypanon.

Lastly, Romance philologists might well notice also that the total number of Greek etyma in REW rose, according to my reckoning, from 182 in the 2d (1924) edition to 775 in the 3d (1932) edition, not counting the learned words bracketed by Meyer-Lübke. This may reasonably suggest that the Greek sources of Romance words may not even yet have been exhaustively explored.

OTHER STUDIES

XXIX

SANSKRIT *GUṆÁ*

Uhlenbeck, *Etymologisches Wörterbuch der altindischen Sprache*, says s. v. *guṇá* (cf. E. and J. Leumann, *Etymologisches Wörterbuch der Sanskritsprache*, Lief. 1, Heft 1, 1907): '... mit mittelindisch *ṇ* aus *n*, vgl. av. *gaonō* farbe[1], np. *gūn*, farbe, art und weise, afgh. *γūna*, haare am körper, poren, farbe, osset. *γun*, *qun*, haare, farbe des haares. Unsicher.'

The important definitions of *guṇá* as stated by the St. Petersburg Lexicon are: '... der einzelne Faden einer Schnur; Schnur, Strick überhaupt ... Insbesondere, ... Bogensehne ... In der Geometrie, die Sehne ... Saite ... Am Ende eines compositi, ... nach einem Zahlwort: -fach, -plex, -πλος (ursprünglich aus so und so viel Fäden d.i. Theilen bestehend) ... Abtheilung, Art ... Eigenschaft (der wandelbare und daher unwesentliche Theil an den Dingen, im Gegensatz zur Substanz), Eigenthümlichkeit ... Eine gute Eigenschaft, Tugend, Verdienst, Vorzug, hoher Grad von ...'

I propose to derive *guṇá* from the zero-grade stem *gu-* of the noun *gó*, 'ox, cow', on the supposition that *guṇá* is primarily an adjective form meaning 'bovine,' whence 'bovine sinew.'

The stem *gó* shows in declension (1) the strengthened stem *gā(u)*, in the forms *gáus*, *gā'vāu*, *gā'vas*, and with loss of the second element of the diphthong, *gā'm*, *gā's*; and (2) the normal-grade stem *gó* in *gós*, *góbhyām*, *góbhis*, *góbhyas*, *góṣu*; *gávā*, *gáve*, *gávi*, etc. That such forms as *gáve*, *gós* are really based on the normal-grade stem *gó* is guaranteed by *góbhis*, etc., and by the inflection of the word in the related languages. And yet, as far as the forms themselves are concerned, *gáve* and *gós* might equally well be from a stem in *u* (like *dhenáve*, *dhenós*, etc.). And in fact we actually find a stem *gu-* in the compounds *saptágu*, 'possessing seven oxen or cows' (*saptágum*, RV 10.47.6), *sugú*, 'having fine cows' (*sugúḥ*, RV 1.125.6), *bahugú*, 'rich in cattle,' *çatagvín*, 'possessing or consisting of one hundred cows', and others. The stem form *gu-* is thus well attested in Sanskrit, tho heretofore only as a final member of compounds; see Wackernagel, *Altindische Grammatik* 3. 1.218f. The ablaut series *gu-*, *go-*, *gāu-* is sufficiently regular in aspect to be an inheritance from prehistoric times, as was suggested by Collitz, BB 10.32. It may be a mere accident that no certain correspondent of *gu-* in related languages is found; cf. however Bloom-

---

[1] Avestan *gaonō* answers regularly to Skt. **gona;* cf. A. V. W. Jackson, *Avestan Grammar* 1. 18. Late Skt. *goṇa*, 'ox', etc., a Prakritic form from *gó*, with lingual *ṇ* like *guṇá*, may perhaps be noticed in this connection.

Reprinted from *Lang.* VI (1930), 36–40.

field's etymology of πρεσβύs, AJP 29.78ff., and Brugmann, *Vgl. Gram.*² 2.1.134. But it is also possible that *gu-* was abstracted from forms of *gó* which coincided with regular *u*-stem forms, such as *gós* ('as if from *gu*', Whitney, *Grammar*, §361 c) and *gáve*; that is, on the analogy of *dhenóḥ*: *dhenú-*, etc. (So de Saussure explained *gu-*, as quoted by Wackernagel 3.1. 219.)

The addition of the secondary suffix *na* to noun or adjective stems to form adjectives is seen in *phalguná*, apparently 'reddish,' and = *phalgú*, *çmaçruṇá*, 'bearded,' < *çmáçru*, 'beard', *çū'raṇa*, if this means 'heroic', < *çū'ra*, 'hero' (çū'raṇa is a ἅπαξ λεγ., epithet of horses, RV 1.163.10); with vṛddhi-strengthening, *straiṇa*, 'woman's', < *strī'*, 'woman'; also, from bases recorded only as adverbs, *viṣuṇa*, 'various', < *viṣu-* and perhaps *puráṇá*, 'ancient', < *purā*. If *dróṇa* ['wooden vessel'] comes from *drú*, 'wood,' it has the anomaly of a guṇa-strengthening' (Whitney §1223 g).² While the examples are not numerous—I omit some possible but less certain ones, mentioned by Whitney—they are sufficient to demonstrate the existence of the adjectival suffix *na* with the value assumed in the derivation *guṇá* < *gu-* (= *gó*) + *na*. Cf. also *goṇa* 'ox', mentioned in footnote 1.

The lingual *ṇ* of *guṇá* may be regarded as of Prakritic (dialectic) origin, as has been suggested by Uhlenbeck (see above). In most Prakrit dialects *n* regularly becomes *ṇ* in all positions of the word (Pischel, *Grammatik der Prakritsprachen* §224). It is well known that in the very earliest stages of Indic speech, even in the Rigveda itself, examples of Prakritic phonology are not rare. For examples, see Wackernagel 1. xviii f.; and further, a paper on 'Dialectic Phonology in the Veda' which Professor Edgerton will shortly publish in the volume of Studies in honor of Professor Collitz. The earliest occurrences of *guṇá* are found in post-Rigvedic texts;³ that is, at a time when the assumption of middle-Indic influence is *a fortiori* entirely plausible. The probability of this explanation is increast by the occurrence in late Sanskrit of the word *goṇa* 'ox', mentioned above; it also has lingual *ṇ*, and is obviously of Prakritic character and origin.

The sense-development indicated is: (1) 'bovine', (2) 'bovine sinew', (3) 'sinew', (4) 'bow-string' (later also 'chord of an arc', cf. German *Sehne*), (5) 'strand, cord (of rope)', (6) 'quality', (7) 'virtue', the last four stages being fully attested in Sanskrit. The passage from (1) to (2), involving a shift from adjectival to substantival function, is analogous to that seen

---

² The connection of *dróṇa* with *drú* is indicated by Uhlenbeck, and seems extremely probable.

³ The earliest case is possibly Taittirīya Saṁhitā 7. 2. 4. 2, where *guṇá* clearly means 'cord, strand' (as constituent of a rope). It is impossible to say whether this is earlier or later than Atharva Veda 10. 8. 43, where the precise meaning is not clear; it may be the same. These seem to be the only occurrences recorded in the Vedic Saṁhitās.

in *sāraghá*, 'honey,' from *sarágh* or *sarághā*, 'bee'. Here the derivative noun is shown by its formation to be primarily an adjective. Other examples might readily be given; but the principle is so well establisht in grammar (see Whitney §1208) that expatiation on this point seems unnecessary.

The close semantic relationship between the notions 'sinew', 'bowstring' and 'cord' is neatly indicated by Latin *nervus* 'sinew, tendon, nerve, ... string of a musical instrument, ... bowstring ...' (Andrews-Lewis-Short, *Latin Dictionary*); Greek νεῦρον 'sinew, tendon [with metaphorical derivatives], cord made of sinew for fastening the head of the arrow to the shaft, ... also, a bowstring' (Liddell and Scott, *Greek-English Lexicon*); and German *Sehne* '(1) sinew, tendon, nerve, (2) string (of a bow), (3) in geometry, chord' (Flügel, *Deutsch-englisches Wörterbuch*).

The semantic probability of the etymology is supported also by the circumstance that the word *gó* is itself used in the Veda to designate various bovine products, and, in fact, anything derived from an ox or cow, precisely as the word *drú*, 'wood, tree,' is used to designate any article made of wood, such as a wooden cup, an oar, etc. In the Veda the word *gó* itself is used of milk, butter, beef, oxhide, and anything made from it, such as reins, whip-lashes, leather thongs, etc.; and finally, it is used several times of the bow-string. See the St. Petersburg Lexicon, s. v.; Grassmann, *Wörterbuch zum Rigveda*, s. v.; Zimmer, *Altindisches Leben* 228; Macdonell and Keith, *Vedic Index* 234. Zimmer and Macdonell and Keith assume that the bow-string referred to simply by the word *gó* (singular or plural) was made of hide or leather. But they are clearly wrong; the bow-string was made of sinew, as is proved by Atharva-Veda 7.50.9, where the word *snā'van* 'sinew', is used of the bow-string: *dhánuh snā'vneva nahyata*.

Since, therefore, the word *gó* itself, literally 'ox' or 'cow', means in the Veda 'bow 'string', and since the bow-string was demonstrably made of sinew, it is evident that one of the meanings of *gó* was '(bovine) sinew'. My attribution of this meaning to the word *guṇá*, and my assumption that *guṇá* was originally an adjective meaning 'bovine', are thus made yet more plausible.

In other regions than India, numerous primitive peoples are known to have made extensive use of sinew for cord, and especially for bow-strings. A description of the process for making bow-strings generally used among the North American tribes is given by O. T. Mason, 'North American Bows, Arrows and Quivers,' in the *Annual Report of the Smithsonian Institution*, 1893. 645: 'The strip of gristle extending from the head along the back and serving to support the former, and those from the lower part of the legs of deer and other ruminants were selected. These were hung up to dry. For making bowstrings the gristle was shredded with the fingers in fibers as fine as silk in some tribes, but coarse in others. These fibers were twisted into yarn on the thigh by means of the palm of the hand, after the manner of the cobbler . . .' Similarly, S. T. Pope, 'Yahi Archery,' *University of California Publications in Archeology and Anthropology* 13.108. The sinew-backt bow, a weapon of many primitive peoples, may also be mentioned as an indication of the extensive use made of sinew for cord among primitive peoples.

The only rival etymology of the word *guṇá*, so far as I know, is that mentioned doubtfully by Uhlenbeck add Leumann, and quoted by me at the beginning of this paper.[4] It seems to me very implausible on the face of it. The Avestan *gaonō* and its derivatives in the later Iranian languages seem clearly to have meant primarily 'hair'; see Bartholomae, *Altiranisches Wörterbuch*, s. v. The meaning 'quality' evidently develops secondarily from this meaning, through the (attested) intermediate stage 'color of hair, color', that is, *external aspect*. On the other hand, Sanskrit *guṇá* comes to mean 'quality' through the meaning 'strand of a rope', and so (*internal*) *constituent element*. Both the inherent probabilities and the actual use of the word in the Veda prove that this is the true semantic development. Since, therefore, the *primary* meanings of the two words are utterly unrelated, the etymology certainly deserves no consideration.[5]

[4] It appears to have been first suggested by Geiger, *Handbuch der Avestasprache* 227 (1879).

[5] On several phases of this etymological study, I have received helpful suggestions from Professor Franklin Edgerton.

XXX
NOTES ON THE PRESENT STATUS OF THE CATALAN LANGUAGE

It is known that the present autocratic government of Spain, in the interest of Spanish nationalism, forbids the use of regional forms of speech in schools. To what extent does this result in the suppression of the Catalan language? Such a question cannot be answered definitely on the basis of the impressions of a summer tourist, but a few observations made in the course of a brief stay at Barcelona may be worth recording.

The entire population seems to be bilingual. While very many of the names shown on shop-signs are obviously Catalan, the language used on the same signs is exclusively Spanish. The inhabitants address one another in Catalan on the street, in street cars and hotels, and at the *frontón*. Foreigners and non-Catalan Spaniards, when recognized as such, are accosted in Spanish.

Notwithstanding the extensive oral use of their local idiom by natives of Barcelona, the preponderance of Spanish in writing and print is unquestionably great. So far as I was able to ascertain, only one of the daily newspapers published in Barcelona is printed in Catalan. Several humorous weeklies are sold at kiosks, and when inspected turn out to be printed in the local language. Taken in connection with the other linguistic facts observed, this circumstance may be interpreted as indicating that even the reading public of the metropolis of Catalonia is actually more at home in Catalan than in the national language.

The recognized classic of modern Catalan literature is *L'Atlantida*, by Jacint Verdaguer, a heroic poem relating the adventures of Hesperis and her rescuer, Hercules, who escaped from Atlantis when it sank beneath the surface of the ocean. Hundreds of books recently printed in Catalan are sold in Barcelona bookstores; e.g., in the Librería de Francisco Puig, 5, Plaza Nueva, whose *Cataleg d'obres de fons*, 1926–1927, contains about 200 Catalan titles. A facil and not unpleasing contemporary writer is Josep M. Folch i Torres, who is advertised to produce a whole novel each month for the Biblioteca Gentil.

The *Diccionari catala-castellà i castellà-català ... per A. Rovira i Vergili*, Barcelona, 1913, is fairly useful. The *Gramàtica catalana* by Pompeu Fabra, 4th edition, Barcelona, 1926, is a standard work published by the Institut d'Estudis Catalans; the same may be said of *Textes catalans avec leur transcription phonétique* .... *par J. Artega Pereira, ordenats i publicats per P. Barnils*....

For a recent discussion of the filological classification of Catalan, see A. Alonso, Revista de Filología Española, XIII, 1926, 1–38, 225–261, controverting views on this subject expressed by Meyer-Lübke and A. Griera.

XXXI

CLOSE AND OPEN *E* AND *O* AT THE CENTRO DE ESTUDIOS MADRID

After a review of pertinent statements appearing in textbooks and in writings of phoneticians, I here present some of the results of auricular observations which I made in the summer of 1927 at the Centro de Estudios Históricos in Madrid, on the pronunciation used by teachers of that institution in their courses for foreigners. The Spanish pronunciations here assembled and interpreted were distinctly heard in the classroom in the courses of lectures or linguistic drill, and the individual words are accompanied by superior letters indicating the teacher who pronounced them in the manner shown. The professors, associate, instructor and lecturer whom I take the liberty of quoting in this way are, named in alphabetical order with the identifying superior letters, Professor Dámaso Alonso,[a] Professor Barnés,[b] Professor Rafael Benedito,[t] Professor Américo Castro,[c] Professor Dantín,[d] Señor Samuel Gili Gaya,[g] Associate of the Centro (in charge of the summer courses in Phonetics and Intonation); Señor Ramón Iglesias,[i] instructor in the Practical Classes; Señorita Maetzu,[m] lecturer; Professor Ovejero.[o]

My previous practical work in Spanish phonetics has consisted in an exchange of lessons with various Cuban school-teachers (1901) and five months' study of Spanish pronunciation in Mexico City (1911–12).

The statements made in textbooks of Spanish concerning the pronunciation of *e* and *o* vary somewhat remarkably. A number of grammars indicate only one sound for each of these letters. Thus, Birch, *Elementary Spanish Grammar*, 1920, says these vowels are sounded as in FATE, NOTE. But Fuentes and François, *Practical Spanish Grammar*, 1916, after saying, "The sounds of the Spanish vowels never vary," state that the letters in question are pronounced as in FAIRY, NORTH. Ramsey, *Spanish Grammar*, 1902, giving the key-words TAKE, HOPE, remarks: "These vowels, although somewhat fainter when not accented, always retain the same character of sound." De Vitis, *Brief Spanish Grammar*, 1922, states that the vowels are sounded as in GATE, NORTH. Passarelli, *Simple Spanish Lessons*, 1926, gives the keywords MET, FORM, adding: "The student will do well to learn *only* the five basic sounds of the vowels. While it is true that *e* and *o* may be open as well as closed, the distinction between their open and close sounds is of much smaller importance than the correct basic sounds."

Reprinted from *MLF* XIV (1929), 22–25.

On the other hand, perhaps a majority of the Spanish grammars in use indicate both close and open sounds for *e* and *o*, but the indications are somewhat varied and conflicting. Thus Clarke and Arteaga, *Spanish Grammar*, 1919, after giving the key-words FATE, NO, say: "The vowels *e* and *o* have a somewhat more open sound when they precede *r* (more rarely *s* and *z*), followed by another consonant; also before *i* in diphthongs and before *r*, *n* final; *e.g.*, *adornar, hospital, hermano, estoy, ley, seis, amor, temer.* Contrast *coro, corro* . . ." Warshaw and Bonilla, *Essentials of Spanish*, 1924, say the vowels are pronounced in open syllables as in TAKE, NOTE; in closed syllables, before *rr* and in the diphthongs *ei, oi*, as in LET, BORDER. Only in this book do I find the statement: "*O* is also open before a single *r*, as in *oro*." Collet, *Méthode active de langue espagnole*, 1920, gives the *o* in French *homme* as the norm for Spanish *o*; Spanish *e* is said to be pronounced as French *é*; exceptionally as French *è* before *r, s, z* in closed syllables. Coester, *Spanish Grammar*, 1917, says the sounds in question are like the vowels in GATE, NOTE; he makes no distinction between open and close *o*, but states that in certain positions, especially before *l* and *r*, *e* is sounded as in MET; examples: *papel, tener, ella, perro, este.* Driscoll, *Spanish Instructor*, 1923, after giving the key-words PAY, NOTE, says that in a closed syllable *e* is pronounced as in TELL; examples: *el, centavo.* Similarly in his *New Spanish Book*, 1925. According to Hills and Ford, *Spanish Grammar*, 1907, "*E* is usually closed, but is moderately open in most closed syllables, or when followed by *ll* or *rr*, as in *él, ser, ten, este, ella, perro*, etc., and very open in the diphthong *ue* (here *e* approximates the French *eu of seul*). Open *o* is the only one that is normal is Castilian. . . . It is more closed after labials (as in *amor*) and in open syllables, but is never so closed as in French *beau*." Wilkins, *Spanish Reference Grammar*, 1923, probably following the second edition of Navarro Tomás' *manual de pronunciación española*, makes the following distinctions: Close *e*, as in CAFE, occurs at the end of a strest syllable, or before *n* or *s* at the end of a strest syllable; open *e* as in SET occurs in closed syllables except those closed by *n* or *s*; also before *rr, j* and in the diphthong *ei*. Close *o* as in OBEY is heard at the end of a strest syllable; open *o* as in ORDER is heard in closed syllables, before *rr, j* and in the diphthong *oi*. Bushee, *Fundamentals of Spanish*, 1927, gives the key-words HEY, HOPE, stating that in closed syllables the vowels are more open, as in LET, NORTH. Torres, *Essentials of Spanish*, 1927, states that the vowels are pronounced as in THEY, OBEY; but in closed syllabes *o* is sounded as in FOR, *e* as in BET, except before *d, m, n, s, z, x = s*. Olmsted, *First Course in Spanish*, 1920, states that in an open syllable, *e* is sounded as in THEY; in a closed syllable, as in THERE; *o* in an open syllable, sounded as in GO; in a closed syllable, as in OR.

Turning now to the phoneticians, I find that Araujo, *Estudios de fonétika kastellana*, 1894, distinguishes four varities of *e*, three of *o*, as follows: very open *e*, as in *puerto*; open *e*, as in *el*, *ser*; close *e*, as in *kafé*; semisilent *e*, as in the last vowel in *trece*; very open *o*, as in *gloria*; open *o*, as in *montón*; close *o*, as in *pote*.

Josselyn, *Etudes de phonétique espagnole*, 1927, finds close *e* and *o* only in unstrest syllables, as in the ultima of *tente*, *huésped*, the penult of *intérprete*, the ultima of *morboso*. Accented *e* is open in the first syllable of *huésped*, *puesto*, *cuento*; more open in *el*, *ser*; intermediate in the last syllable of *tenté*. Josselyn finds hardly any difference among the accented vowels of *solo*, *gloria*, *mono*, *amor*, which he would like to call intermediate—*moyennes*.

Colton, *La Phonétique castillane*, 1909, with complications and variants which cannot be clearly shown in a terse statement, distinguishes four grades of *o*-sounds and four principal grades of *e*-sounds. I will endeavor to summarize these distinctions. First *o*-sound: close *o* as in *sola*, *paso*, *ro:ja*, the first vowel in *ho·nor*. Second *o*-sound: the less close *o* in the ending *-ion*, and in *pote*,[3] which is also pronounced with the third *o*-sound, pOte. This third *o*-sound, half-open, is heard in *lOs*, *mOzo*, the first vowel of cOnocer, and in *bOsque*, which is also pronounced with the fourth *o*-sound, *bosque*.[1] This last *o*-sound is heard also in *cortés*, *pollo*, *torre*.[1] The first *e*-sound is close as in *te·la*, or *te:la*, *me·sa*. The second *e*-sound is less close, as in the first vowel of *ejemplo*,[3] the second vowel of *Si*, *señor*,[3] and in the pronoun *les*,[3] which is also pronounced with the third *e*-sound, the intermediate or half-open vowel of *pEro*. *Pero* is also pronounced with the open or fourth *e*-sound, heard in *ser*, *el*, *pue·de*, *vie:ne*.[1] Colton asserts that close vowels before a single consonant in the accented penult are due to the closing influence of an *o*, or especially in *a*, in the ultima, as in *E:va*, *e:co*^{2} or *e:co*^{3}; but this theory appears to have been refuted by Navarro Tomás, *La metafonía vocálica y otras teorias del señor Colton*, in *Revista de filología española*, X, 1923, p. 26–56.

The leading authority on the pronunciation of Spanish nowadays is undoubtedly Professor Navarro Tomás of the Centro de Estudios Históricos, whose *Manual de pronunciación española*, the third edition of which appeared in 1926, is beginning to influence Spanish grammars, as has already been indicated. According to this treatise, close *e*, a sound less tense and close than the corresponding vowel in French *chanté*, German *fehlen*, occurs in open accented syllables, as in *pecho*, *sello*, *peña*, *compré*, *saqué*, *queso*, *cabeza*; and in syllables closed by the consonants *m*, *n*, *s*, *d*, *z*, or *x* preceding another consonant, as in *pesca*, *desdén*, *atento*, *vengo*, *césped*,

---

[1] Open sound indicated.
[2] Close sound indicated.
[3] Half-close sound indicated.

huésped, extenso, explicar, compadezco, anochezca, pez. It is pointed out by Hills, *Hispania* 1926, vol. IX, page 364, that the second edition mentioned only *n* and *s* in this connection. Open *e*, approximately identical with the English vowel in *let*, is used in the following positions: (1) when preceding or following *rr*, as in *perro, guerra, regala, guerrero*; except when between *rr* and *s*, an in *resto, resma, correspondí*, where the influence of the *rr* is neutralized by the *s*, a close *e* resulting; (2) before *j*, or *g* sounded as *j*, as in *teja, lejos, oveja, oreja, privilegio, colegio, dejar*; (3) in the diphthong *ei*, as in *peine, seis, veinte, ley, aceite, deleitar*; (4) in syllables closed by any other consonants than *m, n, s, d, z*, and when preceding *x* pronounced as the voiced velar fricative plus the sibilant, as in *verde, cerner, belga, papel, afecto, concepto, sección, técnica, concepción, eximio, exhalar*. Unaccented *e* often becomes relaxt and vague in ordinary conversation, especially when between a strong and a secondary stress, or when final before a pause, as in *húmedo, lóbrego, hipótesis, tómela, mecedor, repetir, conceder, llave, siete, noche, jueves, parten, carmen, López, catorce*. Close *o*, a sound less close than the corresponding French and German vowels, occurs in open syllables carrying a principal or secondary accent, as in *llamó, recibió, boda, moda, pollo, olla, coche, hoyo, adobe, hermoso, decoro, esposa, soñar, bodega, moral, cocido, posada*. The accented *o* of words like *ahora, batahola*, mentioned below, is excepted. A sound similar to the French and German open *o* is heard in the following cases: (1) in contact with a preceding or following *rr*, or its equivalent, as in *corro, torre, roca, rosa, correr*; (2) before the voiceless velar fricative spelled *j* or *g*, as in *hoja, manojo, mojar, escoger*; (3) in the diphthong *oi*, as in *estoico, heroico, doy, soy, voy, hoy, estoy*; (4) in syllables closed by any consonant, as in *sordo, golpe, costa, conde, dogma, portero, costura, adoptar, indocto, favor, sol, razón, boj, dos*; (5) in the accented position, between a preceding *a* and a following *r* or *l*, as in *ahora, la hora, batahola, la ola*. When unaccented, at the end of a word before a pause or between two strong syllables, the articulation of *o* becomes in ordinary conversation relaxt and vague, as in *castigo, muchacho, queso, adorar, temporal, redomado, ignorancia, símbolo, época*.

In connection with these clear, easily learned rules, I will mention the fact that when attacking Colton's theories in the article[4] already referred to, Navarro Tomás recorded notations made by himself and two other scholars, Professors Millardet of Montpellier and Américo Castro, showing three shades (*matices*) of close *e*. However, inasmuch as the above named scholars themselves differed somewhat in their notations, and as Navarro Tomás has disregarded these distinctions in his *Manual de pronunciación*, I shall take no further account of them in the discussion of the phonetic

[4] *La metafonía vocálica y otras teorías del Sr. Colton. Revista de filología española,* X, 1923, p. 26–56.

data which I obtained last summer at the Centro de Estudios Históricos, but shall use the simpler phonetic categories of the *Manual*.

I now present those data, set down last summer, as has been stated, in the classrooms of the Centro at Madrid. The preceptors of that institution do not conform very closely to the norm set forth in Navarro Tomás' book, but show a greater diversity of vowel-quality than he recognizes in the *Manual*.

Thus, while accented *e* in open syllables is generally close, it is often open, for example in *pueblo,^{i} piedra^i* (close or open *e*),^{i} *quieto,^{i} quiebra,^{i} el olor,^{i} parece,^{ie} epoca,^{ec} quisiera,^{o} tiene,^{b} sujeto,^{a} objeto,^{a} equis,^{g} seco.^{d}*

When followed by *m* plus consonant, accented *e* seems to be regularly pronounced with the open sound, as in *tiempo,^{ibg} ejemplo.^{go}* I listened carefully for the closed sound indicated by Navarro Tomás, but failed to hear a single instance of it.

In the case of *n* plus consonant, my data are quite analogous, the sound heard being decidedly open to my ear. Examples: *defiende,^{i} céntrico,^{i} reteniéndole,^{i} haciendo,^{i} reverencia,^{i} vergüenza,^{i} dentro,^{i} fuente,^{i} siento,^{i} sientes,^{i} nuevamente,^{i} acento,^{i} gente,^{i} monumento,^{o} influencia,^{o} mientras,^{b} contenta,^{g} temperamento,^{g} lento,^{i} acento,^{i} cincuenta.^{i}* The fact that all but five of these examples are credited to Señor Iglesias is doubtless due merely to the circumstance that I was assigned to his section of the Practical Classes, and so was able to observe his pronunciation at close range. On one occasion, this instructor remarkt that the vowel in *bien*, preceding a pause in the text read, should be pronounced close, and he did pronounce it so in that one case, but elsewhere he certainly pronounced the same word, analogously situated, with the open vowel, as when reading the sentence *No lo piensas bien* (Navarro Tomás, *Pronunciación española*, p. 233).

When preceding *s* in a closed' syllable, the vowel *e* strikes my ear sometimes as an open, sometimes as a close vowel.[5] Examples of the close sound, agreeing with the rule formulated by Navarro Tomás: *después^{bm}†* beside *después,^{io}‡ es^{ci}†* beside *es,^{g}‡ este,^{i} esta,^{b} esto,^{m}†* beside *este,^{io} estos,^{o} muestra.^{m}‡* Examples of the open sound, violating the rule, are, in addition to the variants already given, *fiestas,^{a} puestos.^{i}*

Examples of the close sound of *e* before *z* preceding a pause, and before *x* pronounced as *s*: *pez,^{i} texto.^{g}*

In closed syllables, *o* is always open. At this point the practice of the

[5] Cf. Colton, *Modern Language Notes*, 1922, XXXVI, p. 235, who, referring to the rule stated by Navarro Tomás requiring the close sound of *e* before *n* or *s* in a closed syllable, says: "The latter cannot be maintained in general."

† Close vowel.
‡ Open vowel.

teachers at the Centro is quite in accordance with the rules formulated by Navarro Tomás.

In open syllables, *o* is generally close, but the teachers of the Centro certainly do not adhere strictly to the rule stated by Navarro Tomás, as the open variety is rather common. I noted the following examples: *boda*[i] (open, also close *o* from the same instructor), *cazadores*,[i] *otro*,[o] *otros*,[o] *boga*,[c] *botes*,[i] *cómicos*,[o] *ocio*,[a] *noche*,[i] *persona*,[o] *tono*,[o] *Soria*,[t] *Quijote*,[c] *hermosa*,[o] *jóvenes*.[o] I noticed also *ahora*[o] with the open *o* required by Navarro Tomás, and *la gloria*[i] with open and lose *o*, a case in which it is not clear whether or not the open vowel is required under the rule calling for open *o* in *ahora, batahola*. As a matter of fact, notwithstanding the intervening consonants, he does transcribe *la gloria* with open *o* on page 285 of the *Manual*.

My conclusions may be summed up as follows: Observation of the pronunciation actually used by the teachers at the Centro de Estudios Históricos shows that while the distinctions made by Navarro Tomás in the *Manual de pronunciación española* in regard to open and close *e* and *o* are for the most part in close agreement with the styles of articulation prevailing in that institution, he is, in my judgment, at variance with usage in his treatment of *e* before *m* or *n* followed by another consonant; further, in the case of *e* before *s* in a closed syllable, as well as in the case of *e* or *o* in open syllables, elegant speakers of Spanish use the open sounds with a certain freedom or latitude which has not yet been clearly defined, and which the Spanish phonetician has not indicated in his important and influential book.

XXXII

THE STANDARD OF CORRECT PRONUNCIATION OF FRENCH IN FRENCH CANADA

On the basis of an investigation which I made in the month of June, 1929, of the pronunciation of French actually used by the educated classes in the Province of Quebec, I attempt in the present paper to point out certain variations which appear to exist between the cisatlantic and transatlantic standards of French pronunciation.

I begin with an indication of the writings bearing on the subject. *The Dictionnaire canadien-français* of Sylvia Clapin (Montreal, 1902), while listing in the preface numerous substitutions and transpositions of letters, and the like, was professedly written in opposition to the propaganda of purists, and makes no clear distinction between rural and popular forms on the one hand and careful, scholarly pronunciation on the other. Various important works on Canadian French, I may here state, deal with other phases of the language than pronunciation.[1] Moreover, the interesting *Etudes sur les parlers de France au Canada*, by (Judge) Adjutor Rivard (Quebec, 1914), deals professedly with popular rather than with cultivated Canadian French. This is also the case with the important philological work on Canadian French by American scholars.[2]

Judge Adjutor Rivard of Quebec may be regarded as an authority on Canadian French orthoëpy, inasmuch as his *Manuel de la parole* (second edition, Quebec, 1928) deals systematically with the pronunciation of French. Another influential book, now somewhat antiquated tho still used, is the *Cours de lecture à haute voix*, by the Abbé P. Lagacé (23rd edition, Quebec, 1923). I studied the pronunciations shown in these books, drew up lists of words in which their indications varied from each other or from those of Martinon, *Comment on prononce le français* (Paris, 1913), went over these lists with several educated French Canadians, and discust various doubtful points with these and other cultivated French Canadians whom I had the good fortune to meet, and all of whose names appear at the end of the present study.

At certain points the norm of correct (European) French pronunciation

[1] E.g., *Zigzags autour de nos parliers*, by L.-P. Geoffrion (3 vols., Quebec, 1925–27); *Bon Langage*, (Montreal, 1928), and *Manuel du bon parler* (Montreal, 1929), by the Abbé Etienne Blanchard.

[2] E.g., *Study of an Acadian-French dialect spoken on the north shore of the Baie-des-Chaleurs*, by James Geddes (Halle a. S., 1908).

Reprinted from *MLF* XV (1930).

is known to be somewhat hesitant or debatable. I refer, of course, to the question of the use of the uvular instead of the lingual *r*, the quality of *ai* in *gai, sais, quai, aimer*, etc., the quality of *a* in *roi, écraser*, etc. Even the lists of words included in the present study show, for example, considerable orthoëpic variations between Martinon and Larousse. Analogous variations exist in Canadian French pronunciation, as is shown in the tables appended hereto. Further, if we define the transatlantic norm of French pronunciation as that form of French pronunciation which admits as correct all the variants of Martinon and Larousse, we find in cultivated Canadian French pronunciation still other variations; and these variations —as is the case in the mother country likewise—often assume rather the aspect of local color than of absolute incorrectness, the philologist and purist are inclined to differ on this point. The divergences between Canadian and European French are comparable, I think, to those known to exist between American and British English.

The intonation of Canadian French is distinctly more level than that of European French. *T* and *d* are palatalized before *i, u*, as in *petit, tu, qu'est-ce que vous dites, ça m' est dû*. The open or medial *a* is less open than in Parisian, except perhaps at the beginning of words; examples: *Canada, amour*. In a final syllable, preceding any consonant except *g-j, r, s* (*z*), *v*, the vowel *i* is pronounst open, as in English *it*. Some educated speakers use *é* for *è* in many words. Educated natives of the Province of Quebec often show all these peculiarities in their speech without being distinctly aware of them. Their language gives, none the less, the general impression of correct French. Much less acceptable to the ear is the mispronunciation of *è, -ais* as open *a*, sometimes heard, for example, in the question *Parlez-vous français?* This popular error is avoided by all well-educated speakers.

Open *i* as in English *pin* is mentioned by Geddes[3] as a characteristic of Acadian dialect. Its general occurrence in the speech of educated natives of Quebec has not been pointed out before, so far as I am aware. Suspecting its occurrence in public addresses delivered in connection with the Marial Congress of the Diocese of Quebec, I drew up a list of words[4] including *turbine, vif, mythe, office, ride, plausible, régime, riche, explicite, prodigue* (pronounst with open *i* preceding the final consonant); also *tige, perspective* (pronounst with close *i* before the final consonant); and presented it successively to five of my informants, who carefully

---

[3] *Op. cit.*, p. 34.

[4] *Turbine, ruine, tige, massif, vif, multiple, mil piastres, mythe, office, parricide, vide, Chine, quinine, platine, poitrine, plausible, perspectif, perspective, principe, équipe, guide, ride, rapide, pyramide, régime, rime, riche, fiche, équilibre, explicite, fatigue, prodigue, gencive, paisible.*

pronounst the entire list of 34 words, so that the presence of the open vowel in the positions indicated was satisfactorily demonstrated and acknowledged with almost entire unanimity by the various cultivated French Canadians with whom I discust this surprising phenomenon. I am obliged to state in this connection that Judge Rivard of Quebec, who courteously interrupted the routine of his official duties in the Palais de Justice to talk over with me the subject-matter of my investigation, and who has not indicated the existence of open *i* in Canadian French, either in his *Parlers de France au Canada* or in his *Manuel de la parole*, holds that a recording machine would show a difference in quality between the English and the Canadian French "*i* court." At any rate, the difference is so slight as to be imperceptible to my ear. Dr. A. Vallée, who is a former president of the Societé du Parler Français au Canada and who speaks English, regards the sounds as identical. I had several of my informants pronounce English words containing open *i* with the Canadian French sound, and the acoustic effect was that of complete correctness. Some of my informants having indicated their belief that the Canadian French pronunciation of *turbine*, *vif*, etc., coincides with the normal French pronunciation of such words, I was particularly pleased to be able to compare the two styles of articulation in Dr. Vallée's office in Laval University. He first pronounst the list of words containing *i* in the position stated, and then called his assistant, Dr. Louis Berger, who was born in Alsace and learned his French in France. Dr. Berger also went over the list, and the difference in vowel-quality shown was perfectly obvious both to my informants and to me.

An interesting question, orthoëpic rather than philological in a narrow sense, incidentally arises. Should the Canadian open *i* be stigmatized as a dialectal defect, to be corrected by education and propaganda? At present the sound is prevalently used, in the conditions stated, by college and university lecturers, preachers and other public speakers. It is deliberately avoided by some French Canadians—few in number according to my observation—including Judge Rivard himself and M. Jules Massé of Montreal, president of the Société du Bon Parler. The former regards it as a negligence, the latter as an orthoëpic error.

Was the open *i* imported from France, or is it of recent origin, due to the proximity of English-speaking people? While this question cannot be answered very definitely on the basis of the facts which I have been able to establish, I am inclined to believe, for the reasons which I shall indicate, that the open *i* probably originated in France. In the first place, it should be noticed that while the open *i* is used, in the positions shown, by educated people, including many bilingual persons, it also seems to be the regular pronunciation of Canadian French monoglots, whose vowels cannot have been influenced directly by the pronunciation of the English language. A traveler in French Canada often hears such words as *dites, vite, dix, six* and the like from people of limited education, such as newsboys, automobile mechanics, etc., and the *i* is in such cases regularly open. In fact, this peculiarity of Canadian French constitutes a considerable difficulty for the traveler accustomed to the close *i*, so that a question like *Voulez-vous de l'huile?* is not likely to be understood by the American automobilist when it is heard for the first time. Secondly, an official of the Province of Quebec with whom I discust the open *i* recalled having repeatedly heard the phrase *l'église catholique* pronounst by university professors at Rouen (Normandy) with open *i* in the last syllable, exactly as in Quebec French. Thirdly, Charles Bruneau, in his *Etudes phonétiques des patois d'Ardennes* (Paris, 1913), p. 159, describes an open *i* heard in dialects of the Walloon region and southern Ardenne. He says it has about the same quality as the English final *i* of *happy, pretty*. It occurs in *pipe, tu dis*, and in final syllables including those of *radis, pays, lundi, parti, mourir*, etc. Fourthly, the *Atlas linguistique de la France* (Paris, 1902–10), maps 110, 857 and 1391, indicates that the quality of the *i* in *Baptiste, mille, vif* varies from an open to a close sound in nearly every northern department of France. I mention this fact last and with some hesitation for the reason that the exact quality of the *i* markt with the grave accent in the maps is not stated in the *Atlas*, and so far as I know has never been plainly described. Under these circumstances we are perhaps obliged to assume that it is generally closer than the English open *i*. However, the indications seem sufficient to justify the conjecture that the Canadian French open *i* originated in France, and is hardly to be regarded as an Anglicism of recent growth.

In the last analysis, to be sure, the presence of the sound may plausibly be attributed to the influence of non-Romance languages containing the sound. Gabelentz, *Sprachwissenschaft*, 1901, p. 269 f., adduces various analogous phenomena indicating that an individual sound may pass from one language into another occupying contiguous territory.

For the other vowels, I went over with several informants a list of some 125 words, beginning with a list showing variations between Rivard's *Manual de la parole*, the *Petit Larousse illustré*, and Martinon's *Comment on prononce le français*.[5] Here, not many systematic variations from normal European French are noticeable. *Taon* is regularly pronounst *ton*, which Martinon declares dialectic. A close *e* regularly appears in *abbage, Paraguay*. Individuals vary somewhat in distinguishing open from close *a* in *classe, gare, écraser, crabe*, etc., perhaps approximately as in France, both sounds being used in each of these words.

[5] See Table 1.

My attention having been called to the *Cours de lecture à haute voix* by the abbé P. Lagacé (23rd edition, Quebec, 1923), I was surprised to find this textbook indicating the pronunciation of close *e* in many words

TABLE 1

	R^1	M^2	L^3	1	2	3	Informants 4	5
taon...............	on	an	an	on	on	on	on	on
escadre............	à	â	à	à	à	à	à	
classe.............	â	â	à	à	â	à	â	â
topaze.............	â	â	à	à	â	à	à	
phrase.............	â	â	à	â	â	â	â	â
écraser............	â	â	à	â	â	â	â	â
baron..............	â	â	à	à	â	â	â	â
barre..............	â	â	à	â	â	â	â	â
gare...............	à	â	à	à	â	à	à	â
crabe..............	â	â	à	à	à	â	à	â
fable..............	â	â	à	â	â	â	â	â
narrer.............	â	à	à	â	â	â	à	â
poêle..............	oi oè	oi	oi	oi	oè	oi	oè	oè
blesser............	é	è	è	é	è	è	è é	é è
territoire.........	é	è	è	è	è	è	è	è
cresson............	é	e cre	è	é	è	è	è	è
terreur............	é è o		è	è	è	è	é è	è
poitrine...........	oi	oi	oi	oi	oi	oi	oè	oi
poitrail...........	o	oi	oi	oi	o	oi	oè	o
Paraguay...........	é	è	wè è	é	é	ué é	é	é
abbaye.............	éi	èi èyi	èi	éi	éi	éi	éi	éi
tetanos............	ò	ò	ò	ò	ò	ò	ò	ò
qu'il ait..........	é	è		è	è	è	è	é
qu'ils aient.......	é	[è]		è	è	è	è	
gangrène...........	ga ca	g	g	g	g	g	g	k
quartzeux..........	dz		ts		ts		dz	

¹R—Rivard; ²M—Martinon; ³L—Larousse.

normally pronounst with the open vowel. I then drew up a third list⁶ with a view to ascertaining the extent to which these words are still pronounst with the close vowel by educated French Canadians. A few words pronounst with close *e* in normal French are included in this list, as well

⁶ See Table 2.

TABLE 2

	Lagacé	1	2	3	4	5	6
dessiner	é	è	é	è	é è	è	è
reconnaissants	é	é	é	è	é è	è	è
sont aimés	é	é	é	è			?
les enfants	é	è	é	è	è	é	?
maison	é	é	é	é	è	é	é
serrurier	é	è	é	é	é è	è	è
bêcher	é	è	è	é	è	é	è
enterrés	é	é	è	è	é	è	è
baigner	é	é	é	é	é	é	é
vaisseaux	é	é è	è	è	é	è	è
adresser	é	è	è	è	è	è	è
s'efforcera	é	é	è	è	é	è	è
laisser	é	è é	è	è	é	è	è
terrain	é	è	è	è	é	è	è
nécessaire	é	è	è	è	é	è	è
souterrain	é	è	è	è	é	è	è
compression	é	é	é è	è	é	è	è
professer	é	é è	é è	è	é	è	è
dessaisir	dé	dé	dé	?	dé	dé	dè
descendre	é	é		é	é	è	è
dessein	é	è	è	è	é	è	è
dessécher	dé	dé	dé	dé	dé	dé	
essuyer	é	è	é	é	è	è	
ressusciter	é	è	è	è	é	é	è
nous verrons	é	è	è	è	é	è	è
vous mettez	é	é	è	è	é	è	è
mêler	é	é	è	è	é	è	è
prêcher	é	é è	è	è	é	è	è
blesser	é	é è	é	è	é	è	è
tressaillir	é	é	è	è	é	è	è
essence	é	é	è	è	é è	è	è
essentiel	é	é è	è	è	é	è	è
elliptique	é	é è	è	é	é	è	è
effusion	é	é è	è	è	é	è	è

PRONUNCIATION OF FRENCH IN FRENCH CANADA

TABLE 2—Concluded

	Lagacé	1	2	3	4	Informants 5	6
Leverrier	é	é	è	è	é	è	è
verrou	é	é	è	é	é	è	è
ferrure	é	é	è	é	é	è	è
ferrugineux	é	é	è	é	è	è	è
terrain	é	é	è	è é	é	è	è
terrier	é	é	è	è	é	è	è
terroir	é	è	è	è	é	è	è
étrenner	é	é	é	é	é	è	è
essor	é	è	è	è	é	è	è
serrer	é	è	è	é	é	è	è
veiller	é	é è	é	è	é	è	è
vieillir	é	é	é	é	é	è	è
siège	é	è	è	é	è	è	è
liège	é	é	é	é	è	è	è
piège	é	é	é	è			
sacrilège	é	é	é	é	è	è	è
solfège	é	é	é	è	è	è	è
privilège	é	é	é	è	è	è	è
treizième	é	é	é	è	é	è	è
traiter	é	é	è	è	è	é è	è
épaisseur	é	é	é	è	é	è	è
laideur	é	é	è	é	é	è	è
mairie	é	é	é	é è	é	è	è
haineux	é	é	é	è	é	è	è
je paierai	péré	é	é	è	é	é	èi
j'essayerai	éséré	é	é	é	é	é èi vulg.	?
je m'aseyerai	acéré	é	é	éi	é	èi	?
rafraîchit	é	é	é	é	è é	è	è
excessivement	é	é	è	è	é	è	è
innombrable	nn	n	nn	nn	nn	nn	nn
immense	mm	mm	mm	mm	mm	mm	mm
illuminer	ll	l	ll	ll	ll	ll	ll
avril (p. 63)	ll (mou.)	il	il	il	il	il	il
paresseux	é	é	è	é	é	è	è

as *avril* and three words containing *nn*, *mm*, *ll*, respectively. The number of cases in which *é* is pronounst by some where *è* is normal is shown by this list to be rather large. Owing to the danger of misunderstanding, I generally repeated each of these words after the informant before transcribing it, so that my interpretation had the approval of the informant in each case. A markt difference among the individual informants is noticeable in the pronunciations indicated in this list. The informants whom I designate by the numbers 1 and 4 generally agree with Lagacé in pronouncing é, while informants 5 and 6 show exactly the opposite tendency, pronouncing è in nearly all cases. In some of the words, particularly *liège, piège, sacrilège, privilège*, the fondness of some French Canadians for é is a recognized archaic trait; but this pronunciation is now rather emphatically discouraged at the Laval as well as at the McGill University, and may at present be regarded as popular or elderly. In *aimés, les enfants, maison, baigner, laisser, descendre*, the é heard from some, or in the case of *baigner* from all of my informants, can hardly be regarded as abnormal. On the other hand the use of é in *terrain, professer, verrons, prêcher, rafraîchit*, etc., while doubtless representing the pronunciation most highly esteemed in France about 75 years ago, when Lagacé was compiling his data, may now be considered a local trait which has already been abandoned by many cultured French Canadians, and may be expected to disappear.

The compilation of the data presented in this study has been rendered possible by the obliging coöperation of the following officers and employees of the Province of Quebec and of Laval University, all of whom have carefully pronounst numerous words at my request for the purpose of indicating the leading features of Canadian French orthoëpy: M. L.-P. Geoffrion, Greffier de l'Assemblée législative, Province of Quebec; Secrétaire de la Société du parler français au Canada; M. C.-J. Magnan, Inspecteur des écoles catholiques, Département de l'instruction publique, Province of Quebec; l'abbé Philias Fillion, Recteur de l'université Laval, Quebec; Dr. A. Vallée, Professeur à l'université Laval, Quebec; M. Cyrille Vaillancourt, Chef de la division d'Apiculture et d'Industrie du Sucre d'érable, Ministère de l'Agriculture, Province of Quebec; Dr. Louis Berger, Professeur à l'université Laval, Quebec; M. B.-O. Filteau, Assistant Secrétaire, Département de l'Instruction publique, Province of Quebec; Mgr. Wilfred Lebon, Professeur de philosophie, Collège de Sainte-Anne de l'Apocatière, Province of Quebec; M. Robert Chouinard, Quebec; M. Rodolphe Fortier, Quebec; M. H.-F. Morissette, Quebec.

Further, useful advice and assistance in this connection has been received from the following persons:

M. L.-P. Geoffrion (see above); M. Cyrille Vaillancourt (see above); M. Alphonse Desilets, Chef du service de l'Economie domestique, Province of Quebec; M. Jules Massé, Président de la Société du bon parler, Montreal; Mgr. Camille Roy, Vice-recteur de l'université Laval, Quebec;

l'abbé Etienne Blanchard, Montreal; Professor R. du Roure, Head of the Department of Romance Languages, McGill University, Montreal; Mlle. Idola Saint-Jean, professeur de diction française, McGill University, Montreal; Professor Paul Massé (of Montreal and) University of Alberta, Edmonton, Alberta; Mme. Luc Dupuis, Village des Aulnaies, Province of Quebec.

XXXIII

CLOSE AND OPEN *E* AND *O* IN CUBA

In my article *Close and Open E and O at the Centro de Estudios Históricos* (*Modern Language Forum*, XIV. 22–25, January, 1929) I showed that instructors at the Centro do not closely conform to the orthoëpic rules enunciated by Navarro Tomás in his *Manual de pronunciación española*.[1]

Seeking further light on the pronunciation of *e* and *o* among well-educated and cultivated speakers of Spanish, in the course of the month of June, 1930, I made a summary investigation of the pronunciation of these vowels in Habana Spanish, going over numerous words with the following persons, whose indispensable cooperation I gratefully acknowledge:

Dr. Juan Miguel Dihigo, Professor of Linguistics and Languages in the University of Habana. (Abbreviation: D.)

Manuel Carnesoltas, Correctional Judge. (Cn.)

Dr. M. Rodríguez Ponce, Professor of Grammar and Spanish Literature, Instituto de Segunda Enseñanza. (R.)

Miss Concepcion Fernández Morales, Sepúlveda College. (F.)

Tomás Montero, Inspector in the Department of Public Instruction, and Editor of El Mundo. (Mt.)

Félix Callejas. Editor of El Mundo. (Cj.)

Reinaldo Díaz Versón, Professor in the Normal School for Teachers; and Reporter for El Diario de la Marina. (DV.)

Tamás Montero, Jr., Reporter for El Diario de la Marina. (Mh.)

Lope Morales, Musician (retired). (Ms.)

Most of my informants were, as might have been expected, at the outset

---

[1] My article was followed in the *Forum* by two essays on the same subject by L. Carballosa. This writer, residing at Berkeley, demands a close vowel in *amor, soy, hoy, hablador, tener, perro, bolsa*, the suffix *—on*; an open vowel in *coro, oro, estoy, voy, saqué, queso, desdén, huésped, extenso, cosa, cosita, velo, velas, teme* (indicative only), *temes, temen,* the suffixes *—ero, —era, —ela,* the diphthongs *ie* and *ue*; further, he says that accented final *e* and *o* are invariably open, and that accented *e* in a prepenultimate syllable is always open. (*Forum*, XV. 67–69, April, 1930.) In the second essay, Carballosa tries to distinguish in pronunciation two series of homographic words: *bota* "winebag" (with alleged open *o*), *bota* from *botar* (with alleged close *o*) and the like. (*Forum*, XVI, 62–64, April, 1931.) This distinction may be compared with the well-known imaginary difference between the vowel in English *fur* and that in English *fir*. Carballosa, perhaps misled by the Spanish-English dictionary, errs fatally in defining the quality of English vowels. While most of the Spanish pronunciations indicated by him are sometimes heard, they are not, I should say, in very general use among Spanish-speaking people.

Reprinted from *MLF* XVII (1932), 103–4.

unaware of the endeavors which have been and are being made to distinguish close and open sounds of *e* and *o* in Spanish, and lay down rules for their occurrence and use. However, after discussion, they were all able to recognize the close and open sounds, and became interested in the philological and orthoëpic problem involved in the distinction.

I now present, with such orthoëpic inferences as seem justifiable in the circumstances, the data which the obliging informants with unanimous cheerfulness supplied, and which, with occasional interruptions for verification or discussion, I set down seriatim in their presence.

I. *E* in Open Syllables

In the preterit indicative (*saqué, compré*) the Cuban informants all use a close vowel, here agreeing with Navarro Tomás; and in the future (*hablaré*) only two of the nine (Ms, R) pronounce an open *e*. And only two (Ms, F) pronounce an open vowel in *café*.

Before *j*, or *g* preceding *i*, the vowel is uniformly open: *teja, lejos, oveja, dejar, colegio*; likewise after *j* (and preceding *t*) in *objecto, sujeto*; in the diphthong *ie*[2]—*quieto, piedra, quiebra, tiene*; in the proparoxytone *época*[3]; before *c* followed by *e* in *parece*; and in the phrase *el olor*.

A close vowel uniformly appears in *ceno, cenas, peno, penas, debo, debes, demo, temas*, and with one dissenting voice (Mh) in *cabeza*. As for *temes, teme* (indicative), eight of the informants make the vowel close, Professor Dihigo alone pronouncing it open, thus distinguishing the indicative *teme* from the imperative *teme*, which, all agree, has a close *e*. The first element in the diphthong *ei*, which Navarro Tomás declares open, has rather the close sound in Cuba. Thus, in *aceite, deleitar*, eight informants (all but D) pronounce a close *e*; in *ley, peine, seis, veinte*, only two informants (D, Cn) use the open vowel; and even they vary in the case of *veinte*. The Cubans pronounce an open *e* in *regla, centinela, primero*, with one dissenting voice in each case (Ms, D, D). Six informants (D, Cn, Ms, Mt, Cj, F) pronounce a close vowel in *pecho*, one (DV) hesitating between the close and open sounds; áve (D, Cn, Cj, F, R) pronounce a close vowel in *velo, velas*, five (D, Ms, Cn, Mt, Cj) in *sello*, four (D, Ms, Cj, F) in *queso* with two (Cn, DV) hesitating between close and open, two (Cn, DV) in *ella*, on (D) in *pueblo*, one (Cn) in *equis*; the other informants using the open vowel in each case.

II. *E* in Closed Syllables

In closed syllables *e* may be said to be regularly open, as is shown by the following examples, in which no variation was observed: *verde, cerner*

---

[2] Here the Cubans agree with Carballosa, not with Navarro Tomás.
[3] Here, too, the rule of Navarro Tomás is quite questionable.

(both vowels), *tener, hermano, belga, papel, afecto, concepto, concepción, sección, técnica, guerra, guerrero, cerro, papel*[4], *céntrico, influencia, reverencia, defiende, después* (both vowels), *resma, compadezco, compadezca, tiempo, ejemplo*. The last fifteen examples, it should be noted, contradict indications of Navarro Tomás demanding a close vowel.

On the other hand, one (Cn) of the informants has a close *e* in *muestra, temer*; one (Cn) in *este, esta, esto*; one (Cj) in *monumento*; one (Cj) in the second vowel of *extenso*; three (Mt, Cj, F) in *fuente*; five (D, Cn, Mt, Cj, F) in *dentro*; eight (D, Cn, Ms, Mt, DV, Mh, Cj, F, R) in *atento, vengo*; eight (D, Ms, Mt, DV, Mh, Cj, F, R) in *bien*; and all without exception pronounce *desdén, sartén* with a close vowel in the second syllable. In the case of *perro*, eight of the informants clearly make the vowel open, but Judge Carnesoltas varies from the close to the open sound.

III. *O* in Open Syllables

In the ánal position, as in *habló, llanó, recibió*, both the close and the open sound are used, with an appreciable preponderance of authority (D, Cs, Dv, Mt, F) favoring the close sound.

Following an initial *r* in *roca, rosa*, and preceding a *j* in *manojo*, the *o* is invariably open, as Navarro Tomás has it; but preceding the accent in *mojar*, the vowel is close in the pronunciation of two informants (Cn, Mh); and in the somewhat analogous *escoger*, four informants (Cn, Mt, Mh, F) have a close *o*.

In the proparoxytone *cómicos*, all the informants pronounce the vowel open, although according to one of Navarro Tomás' rules it is close; and in another proparoxytone, *jóvenes*, the open vowel has a preponderance of authority (D, Cn, Ms, DV, Mh, Cj.)

Preceding the accent, *o* is pronounced close without variation in *soñar, bodega, moral*; but divergence appears in *cocido*, which only four of the informants (D, Cn, Ms, F) pronounce with a close *o*; and in *posada*, wherein only five (D, Cn, Ms, F, R) articulate a close *o*; the other informants using the open vowel in each case.

In agreement with a minor rule suggested by Navarro Tomás, we have, in the articulation of eight of the informants (D, Cn, Ms, Dv, Mh, Cj, F, R), an open *o* in *ahora, la hora, la ola*, where an *o* in an open syllable preceding *l* or *r* is immediately preceded by the vowel *a*. However, as I suspected when assembling data on the pronunciation of *e* and *o* at the Centro de Estudios Históricos in 1927, Cuban usage largely conflicts with

---

[4] The plural *papeles* is pronounced with a close vowel by two informants (D, Cn); with an open vowel by the other four (Ms, Mt, DV, Mh) questioned on this point. Here, the close vowel seems due to the openness of the syllable; the open vowel, to the analogy of the singular *papel*.

one of the Castillian phonetician's major rules: the one requiring a close *o* (with a few definite exceptions) in open syllables. We have seen above that in cultured Cuban speech a considerable variation exists between the close and the open *e* in open syllables. In the case of *o*, the variation is more marked, and quite easily demonstrated. According to my perception, all of the informants have an open *o* in *ocio, mozo, noche*; six of them (D, Cn, Ms, DV, Ms, Cj) in *boga*; seven (D, Cn, Ms, DV, Mh, Cj, R) in *boda, moda*; eight, (D, Cn, Ms, Dv, Ms, Cj, R) in *Quijote*; seven (Cn, Ms, Mt, DV, Mh, Cj, R) in *coche*; five (Ms, DV, Mh, Cj, F) in *botes*; five (D, Cn, Ms, DV, Cj) in *otro*; seven (D, Cn, Ms, DV, Mh, Cj, F) in *hermoso, herosa*; six (Cn, Ms, DV, Mh, Cj, R) in *esposa*; seven (D, Cn, Ms, Mt, DV, Mh, Cj) in *cosa, cosita*; seven (D, Cn, Mt, DV, Mh, Cj—Ms varies) in *coso, coses, cose* (indicative), *cosen*; six (Cn, Mt, DV, Mh, Cj—Ms varies) in *cose* (imperative)[5], *cosa, cosas*; five (Ms, Mt, DV, Mh, Cj) in *cazadores*; three (Ms, Mh, Cj) in *habladora*; six (Cn, Ms, DV, Mh, Cj—Mt varies) in *oro*; seven (Cn, Ms, Mt, DV, Mh, Cj, R) in *coro*; five (Cn, Ms, Mt, Mh, Cj—Mt varies) in *adoro*; six (Cn, Ms, DV, Mh, Cj—Mt varies) in *sonoro*; six (D, Cn, Ms, DV, Mh, Cj) in *jóvenes*. Eight of the informants (all except D) articulate an open *o* in *hoy, soy, voy, estoy*. Professor Dihigo uses a close vowel in these words.[6]

IV. *O* in Closed Syllables

In closed syllables *o* is regularly open, as Navarro Tomás indicates. In the following examples, no variations from this useful rule were noted, *hospital, adornar, pertero, sordo, golpe, costa, costura, conde, dogma, indocto, adoptar, torre, corro, sol, razón, hombrón* (both vowels). One word ending in *r*, namely *favor*, likewise follows the general rule. But in *amor, hablador*, two of the informants in each case (Cn, Mt and D, Mt respectively) make the *o* close, perhaps owing to the influence of the plural. Four (Cn, DV, F, R) of the informants distinguish the vowels of *hablador, habladora* as open and close respectively, unconsciously following the rule stated by Navarro Tomás; the other five informants make no distinction between the two vowels in question; and of these five, three (Ms, Ms, Cj) make both vowels open, two (D, Mt) make both vowels close.[7]

In short, cultured Cubans use open vowels, with very few exceptions, in closed syllables. In open syllables, usage varies remarkably, though some of the variations are plainly due to conflicting analogies.

[5] Carballosa's distinction betweens *cose* (indic.) and *cose* (impve.) is recognized by D only.

[6] Carballosa's distinction between *hoy, soy* (close vowel) and *voy, estoy* (open vowel) thus appears to be unknown in Cuba.

[7] The two last-named informants agree with Carballosa.

The extent of regional or national variation in the pronunciation of Spanish *e* and *o* is not definitely known. P. Enriquez Ureña, *Rev. de fil. esp.* XVII (1930), 283, says that open vowels are most prevalent in the West Indies and Andalusia; close vowels in Argentina, Uruguay, and central and northern Spain. The question evidently deserves further investigation.

XXXIV

THE ACCENTUATION OF SPANISH VERBS WITH INFINITIVE IN -*IAR* AND -*UAR*

The difficulty confronting the student of Spanish who is required to write or pronounce in the singular of the present indicative or subjunctive verbs ending in -*iar* and -*uar* in the infinitive, has not been fully met by grammarians and lexicographers. Hanssen, in his *Spanische Grammatik* (1910), p. 64, devotes only a few words to the subject. I find no information at all on the matter in Menéndez Pidal's *Gramática histórica*, the grammar of the Spanish Academy (1924), or Bello's grammar revised by Cuervo (1925). The dictionaries of the Spanish Academy and of Larousse indicate the correct forms only occasionally and incidentally, by using them in definitions. For instance, the Academy, in defining the word *conciliador*, uses the words *que concilia*; and under *gloriarse* it gives the example: *El padre se gloria de las acciones del hijo*. The American grammars, for example Ramsey (1902), Manfred (1923), Hamilton and Van Horne (1925), Hills and Ford (1928), García-Prada and Wilson (1932), and House and Mapes (1932), state rules and present lists of common words with an indication of the accentuation used; but neither the rules nor the lists are in any case entirely adequate and satisfactory for the advanced student.

I find that House and Mapes have the best rules on the subject, including the statement that verbs in -*uar*, except those in -*guar*, have a written accent on the stem-accented forms. If we now add to the exceptions the verbs in -*cuar*, particularly the common word *evacuar* and the technical term *licuar* 'to liquefy', an expression used in smelting, we have a complete and simple rule for the accentuation of all verbs in -*uar*, conveniently replacing the list of 26 words bearing a written accent on the *u*, which appears in Hills and Ford.

However, Hills and Ford give a much more complete treatment of the verbs in -*iar* than any other. They present a list of 42 words in which the *i* bears an accent in the stem-strest forms.

I have recently compiled, and present herewith, a rather extensive list of the verbs in -*iar*; indeed, I have tried to include in it all the verbs in -*iar* recognized by the Spanish Academy in its dictionary; and I have indicated for each verb, in so far as my knowledge and resources have thus far permitted, the proper accentuation in the third person singular of the present indicative. In a considerable number of cases, all of which are explicitly

Previously unpublished. Read before Spanish section of North Carolina Teachers' Association in April 1933.

indicated in the list, the spellings given have been copied (sometimes with the assistance of a reading-glass to determine the presence or absence of the accent) from the dictionary of the Academy or that of Larousse, or in a few cases from a work of Pardo Bazán, *El Lirismo en la poesia francesa*.

My original list of 191 verbs, compiled before I had noticed the Hills and Ford list, was transmitted, a short time ago, to my friend Tomás Montero, an editor of *El Mundo*, a daily newspaper of Habana, Cuba, with the request that he verify or correct the accentuation, particularly that of certain words about which I was in doubt. Señor Montero very obligingly reviewed the list, answering various queries, marking several rare or regional words "desconocido", and making various pertinent comments, which I have entered in the list under the words concerned.

Since receiving Señor Montero's interesting and helpful contribution, I have added to the list various words from Hills and Ford's list, along with many others which I was able to pick out in a second perusal of the entire Spanish dictionary; so that the total number of verbs included is now 246. Perhaps quite a number have still been inadvertently overlookt. In connection with the compilation of the list, I have been able to add 19 words to the Hills and Ford list of words in *-iar* strest on the *-i*. I am, accordingly, appending to my original list, with its appendix, an approximately complete enumeration of the Spanish verbs in *-iar* which are strest on the *-i-* in the stem-accented forms.

In connection with individual words, I will point out that Sr. Montero agrees with Hills and Ford in accenting *vacía*, altho both the Academy and Larousse print *vacia*, without accent. The academy, for example, prints the unaccented form *vacia* three times under the words *vaciador* and *vaciante*. And Benot, in his *Principios de la acentuación castellana* (1888), p. 169, mentions the variant stresses *váciese* and *vaciese*, which he says are well attested in poetry. It thus seems appropriate to affirm that in the case of this word, usage certainly varies. Further, I have noted the stress *expatría* mainly on the authority of Pardo Bazán, *El Lirismo en la poesia francesa*, p. 151, but my friend Montero has silently approved this and also the form *repatría*, which I set down merely on the analogy of *expatría*, I have recently found the accentuation *repatría* in Larousse, where it appears in an example, altho the accent can hardly be made out without a magnifying glass. The list shows that Sr. Montero gives the stress *espacía*, while the word appears in the Academy's dictionary in the form *espacia*. Possibly usage varies in this case, as in that of *vacia*. However, Sr. Montero also indicated the pronunciations *inventaría* and *auxilía*, and I am inclined to believe that this was due merely to a misinterpretation of Benot's work, to which my friendly Cuban informant kindly referred me. I find that Benot places a point under the second *i* in *auxilio, inventario*, which he distinguishes from *auxilio, inventario*, printed without diacritics. But the subpoint, unaccompanied by the usual accent-sign, never indicates stress in Benot's work. The point merely means that *auxilio, inventario* may be read in four and five syllables respectively. I have, accordingly, omitted the stresses *auxilía, inventaría* from the list. The latter pronunciation, anyway, would be liable to confusion with the conditional of *inventar*, and thus violate a principle which Montero himself states in connection with the word *sumaria*, compare also his remarks on *salaria, presidia*.

In conclusion, I would point out that, in the interest of facilitating the study of Spanish in nonHispanic countries, the Spanish Academy might well, in some future edition of its dictionary, indicate the first person singular of the present indicative for all verbs in *-iar*.

[The mimeographed list which was distributed at the reading of this paper has not been reproduced here.]

XXXV

THE PRONUNCIATION OF *E, O,* AND *S* IN CULTIVATED ITALIAN

Regional variation of cultured pronunciation occurs in all languages. The standardization of pronunciation among the cultured classes has gone farthest in France, the Spanish-speaking countries and the United States; while the German-speaking countries and the British Isles have not progrest so far toward uniformity. The difference thus roughly stated is evidently due to the diverse social conditions which, in the course of modern history, have tended, more or less strongly in the different countries, to obliterate dialects.

Italian orthoëpy, cristallized in the dictionaries of Petrocchi, has hitherto been understood to represent the best Tuscan usage, with certain substitutions, particularly the use of *ǧ* for *ž*, *č for š* as in *pagina, pace.* Now, it is very difficult for a nonTuscan to acquire the dictionary pronunciation of *e, o, s* and *z* (*zz*) in all words. Consequently thousands of educated Italians, indeed surely a large majority, are constantly more or less at variance in this regard with the Italian dictionary; and certainly much more in this regard than in any other. In nonacademic circles, at least, the lexical diacritics are often ignored, and the assertion is sometimes heard that the traditional distinction between open and close vowels, and between voiced and voiceless *s, z* and *zz*, are practically negligible except for distinguishing between homographic words of different meanings. This opinion is held, for example, by my friend Dr. M. Puglisi, a writer, editor, and publisher (born in Sicily) residing in Rome. The opposite view, according to which the traditional distinctions should be carefully observed and inculcated, is stated in one form or another by the authors of all the Italian grammars I have seen; *e. g.*, Goidànich (*Grammatica italiana*, 3rd ed., 1931-X), Ferrari (*Grammatica italiana*, 2nd ed., 1919), Fornaciari (*Grammatica della lingua italiana*, reprinted, 1931), Panzini (*Grammatica italiana*, 3rd ed., 1931); and most emphatically by Petrocchi (*Grammatica della lingua italiana*, 1920), who devotes as many as 27 pages to rules for the pronunciation of *e, o, s,* and *z,* reinforced by the following statement (p. viii): "Potrà darsi che nell'educazione di certuni, il dir per esempio *Bozzolo, Zio, Zucchero, Mese, Chiesa, Sposo* colle zete e gli esse dolci o aspre sia perfettamente lo stesso, ma non passerà molto tempo che parrà rozzezza, e visto che nella pronunzia retta di queste parole c'è anche la

---

Previously unpublished. Read before "Italian I section" of the MLA on December 29, 1932.

ragione etimologica, vorrà parere, mi sia permesso dirlo, anche mancanza di cultura".

Nicolà Zingarelli's *Vocabolario della lingua italiana*, 4th ed., 1931, is likely to become influential in Italian schools, as it is dedicated to Mussolini and bears on the cover in the bookshops a commendatory note from the Head of the Government. Zingarelli's marking implicitly contradicts Petrocchi's in *angoscia, canestra, canestro, colpa, colpo, complico, debito,* 'due', *difetto, discreto, enorme, gregge, grezzo, procombere, scrofa*. In the case of *difetto*, to be sure, the indication of close *e* seems merely erroneous. However, Zingarelli varies from Petrocchi also in allowing either close or open vowel in *compito, compra, compro, debito* 'debt', *dopo, gotta, grotta, lamento,* I lament', *mestica, senza*. A careful comparison of Zingarelli's markings with those of Petrocchi would probably reveal various other contradictions or allegedly permissible alternative pronunciations. In the case of *senza*, Petrocchi notes the rival pronunciation with open *e*, but only as a *popular* variant. Somewhat similarly, Petrocchi indicates that the strest vowel of *posto* is close, while Zingarelli says: "*pòsto*, fiorentino *pósto*". It thus appears that Zingarelli's orthoëpic standard for the quality of *e* and *o* does not coincide with Florentine usage; and that he prefers or marks as permissible some pronunciations which have hitherto been regarded as popular or incorrect.

The list of orthoëpic or phonic variations from Petrocchi presented below indicates pronunciations heard from lecturers at the University for Foreigners at Perugia in the summer of 1932, whose names and official positions, together with abbreviations identifying them in the list, appear at the end of the present article.[1] The notations here transcribed were set down in the Corso di Alta Cultura and the Corso per i Maestri; the latter conducted by Professor Enrico Pappacena, a Neopolitan who uses the voiceless intervocalic *s* in a multitude of words, not all of which are shown in the list, and who also pronounced with voiced *z assunzione, attenzione, balza, diplomazia, funzione, invenzione, menzogna, mentione, pazze, sanzione, senziente,* as the voiceless *z* (*zz*) in *grezza, italianizzare, Manzoni, romanzo*. I have not listed this eccentric pronunciation of *z* below, for the reason that nearly all the other lecturers exactly agreed with Petrocchi at this point. One of the teachers at Perugia whom I did not hear, Professor M. D. Busnelli, in his *Guida per l'insegnamento pratico della fonetica italiana* (Perugia, 1931), p. 32, says: "Gl' italiani settentrionali pronunziano sempre dolce l'esse intervocalica delle parole non composte. Quindi anche *càṡa, còṡa, coṡì, naṡo, -oṡo, -cṡia, -oṡità*; pronunzia non perfetta, ma ammissibile, purché il raddolcimento non sia esagerato". This "northern" pronunciation of intervocalic *s* decidedly prevailed at Perugia, even among the Tuscan lecturers; and no speaker whom I had the privilege of observing

[1] [This key was not supplied.]

fully,[2] agreed (in practice) with Petrocchi in this regard. I was given to understand that Professors Papino and Supino, as well as the Etruscologists Neppi Modona and Nogara, are natives of Tuscany. They regularly use the sounds š and ž for č, ǧ in lectures, as does also the Reverend Professor Pietrobuono of Rome even in reading Dante. Professor Boccolini, a native of Umbria, regularly uses ié for iè (as in *pietra*); and so, among others, does Professor Pappacena, who in his lectures casually mentioned this as a southern regionalism. The clear and vigorous speech of Professor Castiglione of Padova showed remarkably numerous variations from Petrocchi in vowel quality.

The total number of words and terminations shown below is 345; of these, 246 entries represent variant pronunciations heard from one speaker only in each case; the remaining 99 entries indicate variations heard from two or more speakers who coincide while varying from Petrocchi. The data were collected chiefly for the purpose of determining to what extent educated Italians violate the difficult rules governing the pronunciation of *e*, *o* and *s*. A dialectological analysis of the variations would require more information than I possess regarding the linguistic experience of the individual speakers. From the orthoëpic point of view, such pronunciations as *béne*, *bréve*, *Gréci* may still conveniently be called "popular". On the other hand, some of the variants shown are so well attested in the use of erudite speakers that they seem to deserve recognition as secondary standard pronunciations; for example, *bisògno*, *brònzo*, *colònna*, *déve*, *dòpo*, *fòndo*, *fòrse*, *-mènte*, *-mènto*, *mòndo*, *nòn*. Perhaps we may include in this category also *caša*, *coša*, *cošì*, *-ošo*, in which the voiced *s*, as has already been indicated, represents a northern regionalism. The list shows that the pronunciation *-ošo* is used by twelve lecturers.

LIST OF VARIANTS

accadèmico Cp
acceša M, C
accešo, accešì Pp
acclusi Pp
affèrma C
agòsto C
alfabèto No
amorètti Pp
analfabèto G
analisi Pp
ancòra C, Pp

angòsto Pp
apoteosi Pp
aquedòtto B
architètto B
Arézzo Su
atteša Cp
autòri C
avèssi Cp, G, M, No

base Pp
battesimo Pi, Pp

---

[2] However, I had an opportunity to discuss this matter briefly with the Etruscologist Buonamici, a native of Florence, whose lectures I was unable to attend; and I found that he exactly agreed with Petrocchi in pronouncing words such as *casa*, *cosa*, *chiuso*, *difeso*, etc.

E, O, AND S IN CULTIVATED ITALIAN 125

Bèmbo Pp
béne B, C, M, Pp
bibliotéca C, M
biéco Pp
bisògno B, Cp, F (also *ó*), NM, Pa (also *ó*), Pi, Pp. (Pc, *ó* regularly.)
bizantinèsco B
Bològna M
bréve C, Cp, M, No, Pp
brònzo Pa, NM, Su
Brunètto Pp
calabraṡe Pc
cartagineṡi No
caṡa B, Cp, NM, No, Pa
caso Pp
céntro B, C, Pc, Pp
cèrca C
céssa C
chiésa B, Cp, Pa, Pi, Pp
chiuṡo C, Cp, Pp
Chiuṡi No
chiuṡura Pp
ciéco Cp, Pp (the latter sounds the *i*)
ciélo B, C, Cp, Pp
circònda Pi
colléga (noun), Cp. (A southern pronunciation according to Pp)
collèghi (verb), Pi
Cològna Pi
colònna NM, Pa, Pp
colòro G (also *colóro*), Pp
còlpa Pi Indicated by Zingarelli (see above); disliked by NM; declared erroneous by Pp and others.
còmpito C, Pp (Preferred by Zingarelli)
complèto Pp
compòsto Pp
(tu) còmpri Pi (Preferred by Zingarelli)
còn Pp
concedèsse No
concètto C
conciso Pp
conclusione Pp
concrèto Pp
confòndere Cp
congèdo Pp
conòscere M
contiéne B
còntro Pi, Pp
conviéne No, Pp
corròtto Pi

coṡa B, C, M. NM, Pa, Pi, Su
cosètta Pp
còrso Pp
costòro Pp
cristianèsimo Pc
cuóre (also *cuòre*), Pp

debolètto Pp
dèdalo M
delusi Pp
deṡignare Bd
dètto No, Pp
déve B, Bd, C, Cp, G, Pc, Pi, Pp
diciottésimo M
diéci M
diétro B
diffòndere Pi
diffuso Pp
dimènticano Pp
disceṡe Su
discréto M
dispòsto No (Allowed by Zingarelli)
diviéne Pp
diviso Pp
dòlce (also *dólce*) Pi
dòno Pp
dòpo B, G, M, Pi, Pp. Disliked by NM; allowed by Zingarelli.
dottòri C
dovèsse Pp

éco No
effusione Pp
egrégia Bd
èmuli C
epentesi Pp
episodio Pp
eroismo Pp
esagera Pp
esclusivamente Pp
esempio Pp
esemplare Pp
èssi M, No, Pi
fantasia Pp
fase G, Pp
filosofia Pp
fisico Pp
fisiologico Pi
fòndere B
fòndo Cp, Na, Pa, Pi, Pp
fònte Pi, Pp,

fòra Pi, Pp
fòrse C, Cp, M, Pi, Pp
francese Pp
frasi Pp
frègio B
frèsco M
frònde Pi
frònte Cp, Pa
fuso (participle), No

gèlo Pp
gènio Cp
gigantèscamente Cp
ginépri Pp
giòrno Pp
giòvani
giovinètta Pp
Giuseppe Pp
gloriòso C
gréci C, NM, No
Grécia C, Bd, No
grémbo Pp

impresario Cp
improvviso Pp
improvvisatori Pp
inchiuṡo C
inchiuṡura C
incompléto M
incòntro Pi
incrédulo B
indiétro Pp
infòndere C
infrònda Pi
ingègno No
ingleṡe Su
insiéme B, No, Pc, Pp
insòmma C, Pi
intèro Pi
intòrno C
invisibile Pp

lavòro C
lègge (noun) No (Indicated in Zingarelli; incorrect according to Pp.)
leggièri B
lènto C
léttera Pp
librètto Pp
lièto Pp
Lándra Su

lòro C
Luisa Pp
luminoṡità Su
luógo Pp

medesimeo Pi, Pp, Z
médico C
médio Bd
-mènte B, C, Cp, No, Pa, Pi, Pc, Pp
-mènto C, Cp, M, No, Pp
mèntre Pp
mercatòri No
métro No
mèsce Pp
meṡi M
metastasio Pp
mèttere C, No
miṡe Su
miseria Pp
mistéro Pp
mòglie No, P, Z
mòlto C, M
momènto Pa, Pp
mòndo Bd, C, Cp, Pi, Pp (also ó)
mònte No, Pi
mòstri Pp
musa Pi, Pp
musica Pi, Pp

nascònda Pi
nascòsto C, Pp
navigatòri C
nòmi M, Pp
nòn B, Bd, M, Pa, Pi, Pp

ògni Cp, F, G, M, Pa, Pc
òltre C
Oméro Bd, Cp
ònda Pi, Pp
ònta Pc
-ònzolo Pp (written -ónzolo on board)
òrdine C
orgòglio Pi, Pp
Orviéto B
-oṡo B, Bd, C, Cp, F, M, Pc, Pi, Pp, S, Su, Z
ottiéne B

pacchètti Pp
paese Pp
paradiso Pi, Pp

parallélo No
parècchie Cp
Pégaso M
pènna M
pensiéro B, Bd, M, Pp
pénso C
permèsso M
permètto M
peśo B
péste C
piédi Pp
piéga B
Piemònte G
Piśa B, No
Piśani Su
piéno B, C, M, Pp (also *pièno*). (Zingarelli marks: *pièno, piéno*.)
piétra B
Piétro B, Pi
poemètto Pp
poémi C
poesia Pi, Pp (also *poeśia*)
poéti C, Pp, Z
popularèsco M
pórgere B
potèssero NM, S
preciso Pi, Pp
préga Pp
prégio Pa
preciso Pi, Pp
prèmi B
presentare G
presente Pp
preśentire B, Pc
préte Cp
problémi Bd, Pp
procéssi C
prodòtti C
proféto B
profòndo Bd, C, Pi
progrésso C
próno Pp
proposito B
propòsto M, No
próprio C

quadernètto Pp
quasi Pi, Pp, Z
quattòrdici B, G (So in Zingarelli.)
quélli M

quèsti M, S, Pi (also é)
quèsto M, No (also é)

raccollèga B
raccònto Pi
rappresénta C
rè NM, No
récano Pp
règno G
residuo Pa
reśiste Cp, Su
reśistente NM
reśo B, Su, Z
rettòre C
ricèrca C
rifòrma C
riliévo B, Pp
rimaśe Su
rinchiuśo C
ripétano C, Pp
ripośo NM
riśolvere No, Pp
rispòndere C, Pi
rispòsta Cp (Zingarelli: *rispòsta; fior. -ó-.*)
ristrètte M
risvègli Pi
ritòrno C, G, Pp
rosa Pp

scèglere Cp, M
scèlta Cp
scéna B, Cp, Pp
sceśe S
schiéro Pp
sciénza B
scóppia Pp
sécoli C, No
secònda Pi
sédia No
sèmbra Cp, M, No, Pa, Pi
sénso C
sentiéro M
sènza Pc (So Zingarelli.)
Siéna B, Pa, Pp
sincéro Cp, Pp
sògno Pp
sònno Pp
sòno B, C, NM, Na, Pi, Su
sòrgono C
sorriśo Pi

sòrsero Pp
sòrta M
sòsta Na
sparó Pp
spécie Pc
spiéga B, Pp
sposare Pi
spòso Pi
spóso Pp
stèssa M, Pp
straniéri Cp
strofètti Pp
studiosi C
suprémo Pp
suso Pi

téma (noun, = 'theme') M, Pp, S
tesori Pp
tiéne B
tòcca B, Pi, Pp
tòmba Bd
Tommaso Pp
tòrna Pp

tradòtto C
tragédic Cp
tramònta Pi
trasmètte Pc

ucciso Pp
umanèsimo Pp
usano Pp
usignuolo Pp
uso Pp
usurpa Pp

valòre C
vangélo Pp
Venézia C
ventolètta (written -é-) Pp
vergògna Pi, Pp
vèrgine Cp
vèro C, G. Z
vèscovo Na
viéne B, M, Pi, Pp
visione G, Pp
viso Pi, Pp

XXXVI

A SKETCH OF THE FINISTÈRE PRONUNCIATION OF LITERARY BRETON

Early in 1937, while planning a tour of Brittany, I wrote to Roparz Hemon, editor of the monthly magazine *Gwalarn*, publisht in Breton at Brest, asking him to let me know how I could best obtain information on the pronunciation of Breton while in Brittany. He suggested that I consult Mlle. M. Gourlauen of Douarnenez, directress of a school for teaching the language by correspondence, or Abbé G. Saout of Saint-Goazec, Finistère. Following this advice in the course of my tour, I spent about twelve hours with each of these obliging informants,[1] both of whom speak Breton as their native tongue, the former using in ordinary speech the Cornouaille dialect current in Douarnenez, her native town, the latter using naturally the dialect of Léon, his native province, altho he is also familiar with the Cornouaille dialect of Saint-Goazec, where he has resided for many years. This involves some mixture of these closely related dialects. Since the language has never been taught in the public schools, and the parochial schools have always been conducted in the dialects, the variations which occur in pronouncing printed texts are naturally considerable. Graphic variations, however, are disappearing, as may be seen by the consistent spelling of *Gwalarn* and of F. Vallée's *Grand Dictionnaire français-breton* (Rennes, 1935), in which the indication of three spellings of the word for 'milk'—*laez, leaz, lêz*—is quite exceptional. An exposition of the pronunciation of Breton, disregarding dialectic divergences, was publisht in 1928 at Brest by Roparz Hemon in a brochure entitled *Distagadur ar Brezoneg*, now out of print. Further attempts to harmonize the differences of the three northern dialects (Léon, Tréguier Cornouaille) will probably be made in the near future, since the Commission de l'Enseignement of the Chamber of Deputies of France, in June, 1937, approved in principle the introduction of instruction in Breton in the schools of Lower Brittany, and requested the Government to put it into effect. At a few points Hemon's rules are at variance with those stated by Vallée (*La Langue bretonne en 40 leçons*, 8th ed., 1932), who recommends that *h* be sounded as in Tréguier, and affirms that certain prefixes are unstrest, adducing (p. 3) as one example *dinerz* 'feeble', which

---

[1] I also observed the reading pronunciation of M. Robert Audic, a resident of Vannes, who, having learned the Cornouaille dialect during his adolescence, pronounces quite like Mlle. Gourlaouen.

Previously unpublished.

according to Hemon (p. 28) is strest on the penult according to the general rule. The most serious difficulty encountered by a nonBreton learner in pronouncing printed Breton is presented by the (largely regional) variations in the sounds of the several groups of vowel-letters, as the rules thus far stated supply insufficient guidance.

The Breton consonants are [p], [b], [t], [d], [k], [g], [m], [n], [ɲ], [ŋ], [f], [v], [w], [ɥ], [s], [z], [ʃ], [ʒ], [j], [ḫ], [h], [l], [l̥], [ɹ] (or [r]).

The explosives are stronger than in French when initial or preceding [l] or [r], weaker when final or preceding other consonants. [f] and [v], said by Hemon to be generally bilabial, are certainly labiodental in the speech of Mlle. G. and apparently in that of Abbé S. Initial w is read as [w] by Mlle. G., but Abbé S. reads it as [v]. [ḫ], spelled *c'h*, equivalent to the German voiceless velar spirant, is sometimes reduced to its phonemic variant [h] as in English *heavy*. According to Hemon this occurs everywhere except in the initial position before *o* when the consonant is not the result of a mutation, and after *r* or *l*: *c'hoant* [ḫwant] 'desire'; *va c'halon* [va 'halǫn] 'my heart'. Neither of my informants pronounced the initial *h* which appears in the spelling of quite a number of words. [ɲ], [ɥ], [ʃ] are pronounced and spelled (*gn*, *u* before vowel, *ch*) as in French. [ŋ], occurring before [g] and [k], is spelled *n*: *engroez* ['eŋgrwes] 'crowd'; *yaouank* ['yawaŋk] 'young'. [ʒ], [j] are spelled *j* and *i* (before a vowel) respectively. [l] loses its voice in the final position following a voiceless consonant. [l̥], spelled *lh*, sounds in reading like Spanish *ll*, tho reduced in common speech to [j]. [ɹ], a uvular fricative, becomes voiceless in the same circumstances as [l]. According to Hemon a trilled lingual [r] is also heard.

The four sets of mutations of initial consonants described in the grammars[2] and indicated by the spelling are made without any error whatever in reading. In some words initial *s* following a voiced consonant becomes *z* (*eur sul* [ø̞ɹ zyl] 'a Sunday'), altho this is not shown by the conventional spelling. The interchangeable consonants [pb], [td], [kg], [fv], [sz], [ʃʒ] are all voiceless when final unless immediately followed by a voiced sound, when they are voiced: *hep gouzoud netra* [ɛb 'guzud ne'tɹa] 'without knowing anything'. This practice is occasionally disturbed by the influence of the spelling. According to Hemon, when two identical or corresponding interchangeable consonants meet in consecutive words, the resulting single consonant is voiceless: *dek gwele* [de'kwe:le] 'ten beds'; *bloaz zo* ['blwaso] 'a year ago'. Hemon also indicates the pronunciations: *levr* [lefr] 'book';

[2] (1) k>g, p>b, t>d, g>c'h, gw>w, b(m)>v, d>z; (2) k>c'h, p>f, t>z; (3) g>k, b>p, d>t; (4) d>t, g>c'h, gw>w, b(m)>v. The type of the mutation varies according to the preceding word which provokes the change. See, for example, the *Tableau des mutations* appended to Vallée's *La Langue bretonne en 40 leçons*.

klask avalou [klask a′valu, klazg a′valu] 'hunt apples', *addeski* [a′teski] 'relearn'.

The oral vowels are [i], [e], its phonemic variant [ɛ], [ɑ], [y], [ø], [ö], [u], [o], and its phonemic variant [ǫ], all susceptible of lengthening under the stress. [ö], pronounced by Mlle. G. in *peoc'h* [pöḫ] 'peace', is a rare sound; Abbé S. pronounces this word [peǫḫ]. [ɑ], as in Breton French, is intermediate between standard French [a] and [ɑ]. In the diphthong spelled *aou* the first element resembles English *u* in *but*, as in *daou* [dʌu] 'two'. [o] and [e] occur regularly in unstrest open syllables; generally also in strest open syllables, these vowels resembling the corresponding Spanish sounds rather than the more tense and narrow French *ô*, *é*. [ǫ] and [ɛ] are generally heard in strest closed syllables, sometimes also in strest open syllables. Examples: *betek* [′bɛtɛk] 'as far as', *klevout a rez* [′klevud a ɹeːs], 'thou hearest', *ret mont* [ɹed mǫn] 'one must go', *hepken* [ɛp′keːn] 'only', *gouestl* [gwestl] 'promise', *dres evel* [drɛs e′vɛl] 'just as, just like', *a-hed ar wech* [ɑ′ed ɑɹ wɛʃ] 'all the time', *straed* [stɹɛːt] 'street', *pa brederie mat* [pɑ bɹe′dɛɹje maːt] 'when she considered well', *beva* [′bevɑ] 'to live', *kêr* [keːɹ] 'city', *hep pec'hed ebet* [ɛp′pɛḫed e′bɛt] 'without any sin', *spered* [′speɹɛt] 'spirit', *kelou* [′kelu] 'news', *aze ne oa nemed eur. . .* [′aze ne wɑ ne′mɛd φɹ] 'that was only a . . .', *ne oa ket eun torfed* [ne wɑ ket φn ′tǫɹfɛt] 'it wasn't a crime', *pegoulz e tlee beza* [pe′gulz e ′tlee ′bezɑ] 'when it must be', *en nevez-amzer* [ɛn ′nevez′ɑmzɛɹ] 'in springtime', *an abreta ar gwella* [ɑn ɑ′bɹɛtɑ ɑɹ ′gwɛlɑ] 'the sooner the better' *dek eur* [deg φːɹ] 'ten o'clock', *skrija a reas* [′skɹijɑ ɑ ′ɹeɑs] 'he wrote', . . . *e krogas* [e ′kɹoːgɑs] 'he seized', *chom* [ʃǫm] 'remain', *chomet* [′ʃǫmɛt] 'remained', *prof* [pɹǫf] 'gift', *noz* [noːs] 'night', *koz* [koːs—kuːs in ordinary Cornouaille speech], 'old', *hogos* [′ǫgǫs] 'almost', *koziad* [′kǫzjat] 'old man', *pok* [pǫk] 'kiss'.

According to Hemon, all the vowels are nasalized when preceding nasal consonants. The easily perceptible nasal vowels are [ĩ], [ẽ], [ɑ̃], [õ], [ỹ], œ̃], spelled *-iñ*, *-eñ*, *-añ*, *-oñ*, *-uñ*, *-euñ* respectively. There is a nasal diphthong [ɑ̃õ], spelled *-aoñ*. [ɑ̃], [õ], and [œ̃] sound quite like the corresponding French nasal vowels. The nasal [æ̃] occurs in French loanwords: *zink* [zæ̃ːk] 'zinc'. Mlle. G. also uses this sound irregularly in *biñs* [bæ̃ːs] 'screw', which Abbé S. pronounces [bĩːs].

The graphic group *æ* is generally read as [ɛ]: *pounneraet* [pune′ɹɛːt] 'made heavy', *kosaet* [ko′sɛːt] 'grown old', *lakaet* [lɑ′kɛːt] 'put' (participle), *taeroc'h* [′tɛɹǫh] 'more violent', *aesoc'h* [′ɛsǫh] 'easier', *aezenn* [′ɛzɛn] 'breeze', *aet* [ɛːt] 'gone', *graet* [gɹɛːt] 'done', *straet* [stɹɛːt] 'street', *er-maez* [ɛɹ′mɛːs] 'outdoors', *aezen-leski* [′ɛzɛn′lɛski] 'gas-burning'. But the group is pronounced [ɑːj] in some words, as in *æ* 'went', *kaer* 'handsome', distinguisht from *ker* [keːɹ] 'dear', *traezenn* 'sand', *krae* 'beach'. *Abardaez* 'evening' was read by Mlle. G. as [abaɹ'da:js] in one passage, as [abaɹ'dɛ:s] in another. When reading *traezenn* with [a:j] she paused to remark that it is probably pronounced with [ɛ:] at Douarnenez. Similarly, Abbé S., when reading *e paeas* 'he paid' as [e 'pajas], stated that this is the pronunciation of Léon, the words being spoken as [e 'pɛas] in Cornouaille.

Mlle. G. reads *abaoe* 'since' as [a'bǫe] or as [a'bʌwe].

The use of the digraph *ou* with the double value of a vowel and a consonant in different words may be illustrated by *sioul* [sjul] 'tranquil', *houarn* ['uaɹn] 'iron', *siouaz* ['siwas] 'alas'.

In the 38 pages of printed text which she pronounced for me, Mlle. G. consistently read the letter-group *oa* as [wa] except in the literary word *hoala* 'to charm'. However, Abbé S. wavered between the [wa] of Cornouaille and the [oa] of Léon, reading *ən doa* 'he had', *koad* 'wood', *oa* 'was', *skoaz* 'shoulder' now with one pronunciation and now with the other. He read *oant* 'were', *oad* 'age', *poan* 'pain' and *warc'hoaz* [vaɹ'hoas] 'tomorrow' with [oa].

The first sound in the letter-group *oe* is generally consonantal—[w]: *ampoent* ['ampwɛnt] 'moment', *engroez* ['ɛŋgɹwɛs] 'crowd', *arboella* [aɹ'bwɛla] 'economize', *loeru* ['lwɛɹu] 'stockings', *goloet* ['golwɛt] 'covered'; but in the imperfect of *beza* 'be' and *endevout* 'have', both readers used dissyllables: [a 'voe] '(he) was', *en doe* [ɛn 'doe] 'he had'. The past participle *roet* of *rei* 'give' was read by Mlle. G. as ['ɹoɛt] in one passage, as [ɹwɛt] in another. When this was noticed, she pronounced forms of the imperfect of this verb thus: 2 sg. *roez* ['ɹoɛs], 3 sg. *roe* [ɹwɛ, 'ɹoe], 1 pl. *roemp* [ɹwɛm], 2 pl. *roec'h* ['roɛh], 3 pl. *roent* ['ɹoɛn]. Similarly, Abbé S. read *troe* 'turned' as [tɹwe] and also as ['tɹoe].

The group *oue* is generally pronounced as a monosyllable by Mlle. G.: *mouez* [mwe:s] 'voice', *pouez* [pwe:s] 'weight', *c'houek* [hwɛk] 'sweet', *roued* [ɹwɛt] 'wheel'; but she read *boued* 'food' as [bwɛt] in one passage, as ['buɛt] in another. Reading *frouez* 'fruit' as ['fɹues], she mentioned that the word is pronounced [frwe:s] in Douarnenez. Abbé S. read this spelling as a dissyllable in *dre douez* [dɹe 'dues] 'across', *kouez* ['kues] 'lye', *inouet* [i'nuɛt] 'annoyed'.

Oui is dissylabic in *toui* ['tui] 'swear'. But *ui* makes one syllable in *echui* [e'ʃɥi] 'to finish' (the past participle is *echuet* [e'ʃyɛt]).[3]

---

[3] In his *Mojennou brezonek kos ha neve ha troïdigez c'hallek* (Saint-Brieuc, 1937), E. Ernault sometimes uses such unambiguous spellings as *rôet* (p. 83), *grêt* (p. 180, 258), *êt* (p. 207), *penôs* (p. 16). The variants *ôtrou* (p. 37), *aotrou* (p. 23, etc.), *tôl* 'stroke' (p. 225), *taol* 'table' (p. 133) appear to be influenced by prosody. In his indispensable *Gèriadurig brezonek-gallek—Vocabulaire breton-français* (Saint-Brieuc 1927), Ernault gives numerous graphic variants indicating the pronunciations used in the four Breton dialects, including the dialect of Vannes, which is so different from the other three that it is not included in present-day Unified Breton (*Brezoneg Unvan*).

FINISTÈRE PRONUNCIATION OF LITERARY BRETON 133

Final consonants are sometimes dropt in reading, tho much less frequently than in normal speech. I noticed *oabl hag heol* [wɑb ɑg eɒl] 'sky and sun', *digabestr hag eürus* [di'gɑbest ɑg e'yɹys] 'bareheaded and happy', *ken dizeblant* [ken di'zeblɑn] (at end of sentence) 'so indifferent', *ar pont bras* [ɑɹ pɒn bɹɑs] 'the big bridge', *an hent heoliek* [ɑn ɛn e'ɒljɛk] 'the sunny way', *hep mont d'an oferenn* [ɛb mɒn dɑn ɑ'feɹɛn] 'without going to mass', *koll he skiant* [kɒl e 'skiɑn] 'lose her senses', *a drugarez Doue* [ɑ dry'gɑɹe 'due] 'thank God'. Mlle. G. reads final graphic -*v* after a nasal vowel in two different ways in different words: *ken kreñv ha ken hir* [ken kɹẽ ɑ ken iːɹ] 'so strong and so long', *eur bagagig merc'hed a-dreñv* [ɸɹ bɑ'gɑgig 'mɛɹhed ɑ'dɹẽw] 'a bevy of girls behind'.

The stress generally falls on the penultimate syllable of words; but there are quite a number of exceptions: Hemon (page 25f.) gives an incomplete list of 67 common nouns and various other words strest on the last syllable. Many of these oxytones are identifiable as compounds: *kenavo* 'goodbye', *kerkent* 'immediately', *kreisteiz* 'noon', *dilun* 'Monday', *gwechall* 'formerly', *nemeur* 'hardly', *netra* 'nothing', *peseurt* 'what (kind of)', *warc'hoaz* 'tomorrow', etc. Inasmuch as the stress in compounds passes to the modifying element, which generally comes last, as in *mamm-goz* [mɑm'goːs] 'grandmother', some of the exceptions—*dilun, gwechall,* among the words just mentioned—are merely examples of this secondary rule. The postpositive demonstrative particles -*mañ*, -*se*, -*hont* 'here', 'there', 'yonder' take no stress, the accent falling on the preceding syllable: *an dra-se* [ɑn 'dɹɑse] 'that thing'. The personal endings added to the preposition *gant* 'with' take the stress except in the 3rd person: *ganéñ* [gɑ'nẽ] 'with me', but *ganti* ['gɑnti] 'with her', *ganto* ['gɑnto] 'with them'. Otherwise the inflected prepositions are regular in stress: *evidoun* [e'vidun] 'for me', *ouziñ* ['uzĩ], 'against me', etc.

A PASSAGE OF BRETON WITH PHONETIC TRANSCRIPTION[4]

Douaret e voe ar vaouez koz eur sadorn   d'abardaez, e miz ebrel,
'dwɑɹet e-voe ɑɹ-'vʌwes-koːs ø ɹ- 'zɑdɒm dɑbɑɹ'deːs, e-miz-'ebɹel,

[4] From *Ar C'hoar Hena*, by Roparz Hemon; *Gwalarn*, No. 48 (November, 1932); pronunciation of Mlle. M. Gourlaouen, transcribed by C. C. Rice.

After my transcription of Mlle. Gourlaouen's pronunciation of the above passage was distributed at the meeting of the Linguistic Society held in Chicago in 1937, the editor of *Gwalarn* was good enough to send me his transcription of his own pronunciation of this extract from one of his writings. In copying his notation I substituted ḫ for his *x*, and ᵘ (superior *u*) for the curtailed *u* which he writes in transcribing *douaret, douaridigez*. He made the following remarks on my transcription and on his own: "Cette transcription de la prononciation de Mlle. Gourlaouen me semble devoir être très exacte, sauf: 'gɹiziĺ (grizilh) qui doit être: 'gɹizij probablement.— J'ai écrit ma propre prononciation. ɒ et ɛ deviennent *o* et *e* (parfois très légèrement ouverts) en Léon."

Buried was the woman-old one Saturday afternoon, in month April,
du'aɹed e-voe aɹ-'vawes-koːs øɹ- 'zaːdoɹn dabaɹ'deːs, e-miz-'eːbɹel
eun devez a varradou grizilh hag a heol nevez-hañv. Eun dwaridigez paour.
øn-'devez-a-va'ɹadu-'grizil̃ ag-a-eol-'nevez-'ãw. øn dwaɹi'diges-'pay̨ɹ.
a day of storms<of>hail and of sun<of>spring.   A burial   poor.
õ̆n-'devez-a-va'ɹadu-'gɹizij ag-a-eol-'nevez-'ã: õ̆n duaɹi'diges-'pauɹ

Ifig hag Herri, diskabell,   a gerze war-lerc'h   ar c'harr noaz, stlejet
'ifig ag-'ɛɹi,   dis'kabel,   a-'geɹze waɹ'leɹh-   aɹ-ḫaɹ-'nwɒːs, 'stleʒed-
Ifig and Henry bareheaded,   walkt   behind   the cart-bare, drawn
'ifig-ag-'eɹi,   dis'kabel,   a-geɹze waɹ-'leɹx-   aɹ-'xaɹ-'noas, 'stleʒed-

gant eur marc'h hepken.   Da heul   e teue Eliza, he gouel-gañv
gand-øɹ-maɹḫ   ep'keːn. da-ø:l   e 'tø:e e'liza, e-'guel'gãw
by one horse   only.   Next   came   Eliza, her mourning-veil
gãn-øɹ-maɹx   ep'ken.   da-'ø:l   e-'tøe e'liːza, e-'guel-'gã:

war he dremm, Jenovefa en he c'hichen,   eur bagadig merc'hed a-dreñv.
waɹ-e-dɹɛm,   ʒeno'vefa ɛn-e-'hiʃen,   øɹ-ba'gadig-'meɹḫed-a'dɹɛ̃w.
on her face, Genevieve at her side,   a small-bevy<of>women behind.
waɹ-e-'dɹɛ̃m,   ʒeno'vefa en-e-'xiʃen,   øɹ-ba'gadig-'merxed-a'-dɹɛ̃:

A-benn eun eur e voe ech'u,   hag an holl war hent ar gêr.
a'bɛn-øn-ø:ɹ   e-'voe 'eʃy,   ag-an-ol   waɹ-ɛnd-aɹ-geːr.
At end<of>an   hour<it>was over, and   all on<the>way home.
a-'ben-'õ̆n-øɹ   e-'voe-'eʃy   ag-ãn-ol   waɹ-ɛ̃n-aɹ'-geːɹ

E kalon Eliza e oa deut eur peoc'h bras.   War he biz e oa
e-'kalon-e'lizã e-wa-'dø:t øɹ poc-'bɹaːs.   waɹ-e-biːẑ-e-wa
In heart<of>Eliza was come a peace-great.   On her finger was
e-'kaːlõ̆n-e'liːza e-wa-'dø:d-øɹ-'peox-'bɹaːs. waɹ-e-'bi-z-e-wa

ar bizaoued-promesa,   roet d'ezi   gant Herri
ɒɹ-bi'zʌwedpro'mesa,   'roɛd-'dezi   gand-'ɛɹi
the ring<of>bethrothal,   given to her   by Henry
ɒɹ-bi'zawet-pro'mesa,   'ɹoe'dezi   gãn-'eɹi

dirak korf an hini   varo.
di'ɹak-koɹf-an-'ini-   'vaɹo.
before<the>body<of>the one dead.
di'ɹa-'koɹv-an-'ini-   'vaːɹo.

WORD INDEX

This index is for the etymological material only. The articles on pronunciation offer many words as examples which it would not be advantageous to list here.

ARABIC
arīr 53
ataṇa 54
basṭa 67
falaḳa 63
fuṭr 72
ḥalaḳa 76
lauḳā' 63
lauke 62
raḳama 63

ARAMAIC
peṭūrota 66, 72

AVESTAN
gaonō 93

BASQUE
abar 46
abarka 46
alarao etc. 53
barau 53
cherria 42
errosca 31
ezker 42
galzarra 75
gaf 77
kia 46
muga 77
mutil 77
su 77
sukaftu 77
txist 80
txistu 78
zerri, txerri 42

CATALAN
abalir 64
abaltir 73
afalagar 76
aise 25
bastar 67
besllum 61
empaitar 42, 43
enconado 74

enconar 74
esqueixar 43, 44
migranza 65
migrarse 65
troll 44
tuf 89

CHALDEAN
garday 10

DALMATIAN
kentra 88

FRENCH
acointier O.F. 71
aisance 25
aise, aisé 25
aller 13, 16, 22, 23, 24, 27, 28
ambler 25
avaler O.F. 64
baste O.F. 67
cointier O.F. 71
écacher 50
empeechier O.F. 42, 43
enciser 49
entoischier O.F. 31
épieu 84
eschafe O.F. 89
espingle 17
estropier 44
fléchir 29, 30, 31
*fleischier O.F. 30
flesche 29
fleschier O.F. 29, 30
genous O.F. 29
gregeos O.F. 7
ivrogne 63
lâcher 29, 75
malaisé 26
malaisier 26
malvaisier 26
mauvais 26
oïl O.F. 47
page 50
pincer 56

por- O.F. 51
potiron 66, 72
puirier O.F. 51
ruche 29
souschier O.F. 46
taster 30, 31
torche 74
treuil 44
trouver 51

GALLIC

*adbalo 73

GERMANIC

amble Eng. 25
*asatia 25
azeti Goth. 25
bit Eng. 31
brauþ Goth. 86
ease Eng. 25
goff etc. Eng. 65
gu- O.E. 93, 94
*lasca Goth. 75
lasch M.H.G. 29
lǫskr O.N. 29
speut Frankish 84
spuits Goth. 84
tanna O.H.G. 54
top Frankish 51
zujagen 10

GREEK

ἀγκών 88
ἄγριος 10
ἄγροικος 7
ἀλουργίς 41
βαθύς 41
βαστάζω 67
βάσχος, etc. 10
γέρδιος 8, 10
γερδοποιόν 11
Greek words in Latin,
 their meanings 88–90
δοῦλος, etc. 10
θάλασσα, etc. 10
θεῖος 41
κάμπτειν 73, 88
κέντρον 88
κλίμα 89
κωφός 65, 90
λιμηρός 90
momos 90

νέομαι 20
νεῦρον 90
νέφω 20
ὄψις 41
πάγη 90
παιδίον 50, 90
πεῖρος 90
πλατύς 36, 88
πρεσβύς 94
ῥαφή 41
ῥύγχος 90
σήψ 89
σιμός 35, 36, 39, 74, 89
σκάφη 89
στρόμβος 89
σχιστός 44
τῦφος 89
φάλαγξ 89

HEBREW

garod 10

ITALIAN

agio etc. 25
alòcco 62
andare 13, 16, 22, 23, 24, 27
barka 46
bastare 67
calcai 18
cansare 73, 74
čentrina Roman 89
consuacero 4
dassari Sic. 59
destare Tusc. 33
falanga Sic. 89
fissare 87
frizzare 50
goffo 65
greggio 7, 8, 9, 10
*grezo 7
grezzo 7, 8, 9
impacciare 42, 68
impedicare 42
inchischiare 49
intoppare 51
leva 31
malagiato 26
malvagio 26
moccichimo 66
moccicone 63
moccio 63

mucca 66
mucco 66
paggio 50
palanca 89
pinzare 56
rogare Pist. 65
rosicare 31, 76
scanfarda Tusc. 89
scheggio 43
sedime 35
sepa 89
sim Canavese 39
spet, etc. Bergam. 84
spitę Neap. 84
storpiare 44
strombo 89
succhiare 31
tastare Tusc. 33
torchio 52
tufo Venetian 89

LATIN

*abballitare 73
*abbrachicare 46
abolēre 64
*adatiāre 25
*addare 12
*ad-de-illa(c)are 28
addere gradum 12
*ad-iterare 28
adnao 18, 24
adnatare 22
adnavigare 21
adno, adnare 18, 19, 22, 28
-agicare 34
*allare 28
alucus 62
ambire 23
*ambitare 12, 23
ambulare 12, 13, 14, 15, 16, 22, 25, 28
*amminare, adminare 15, 22, 23
*ammulare 15
ancōn 88
annatare 16, 21
*annitare 16, 21, 22, 24, 27, 28
*annulare 16, 21, 22, 23, 24, 27, 28
ansa 25
-arellu 66, 72
*atiare, etc. 25, 26
*bag- 42, 43
ballare 73

barca 46
basium 41
*bastus 67
*bathus 41
bĭslumen 61
*bombacius 41
bombyceus 41
c > g after re- 75
caedere 49
caesus 49
campsare 73, 74, 88
campus 73
centrum 88
cerda 41
*cinctulare 54
*cingulare 54
cinis 48
cinisculus 49
*ciniscus 48
cīrcĭtare 12, 24
circulare 12
circumsecus 32
cirrus 42
*cīsicare 49
clima 89
coactare 83
*coacticare 50
*coaxare 83, 87
colluminare 60
columen 60
columna 60
*comptiare 81
conari 74
*consanguinare 6
consanguinitare 6
consecrare 4
considerare 61
consocerum 4
corro 62
corvus 9
crepitare 12
*crepitiare, *re-crepitiare 71, 80
crepulare 12
crovus 9
-cty- 50, 58
culminare 60
*dao 18
*daxare 55
decedere 56
*decessare 55
*de-ex-patt-iare 43, 67

*deexpedire 55
*deextorticare 74
*de-exturpare 44
*deictare 55
dejectare 55, 58
*dejectiare 56, 58
dejectus 58
*dejexare 58, 59, 80, 87
*dessar 56
*de-ex-scidiare 43
*dexare 59
*directiare 58
*disturpare 44
*ebrionia 63
enatare 20, 21, 22, 28
enavigare 20, 21, 22
*estrusulare 45
*excoactare 50
*excostiare 43
*expavitare 73
expīrare 86
*exquintiare 43
*extorpidare 44
extrinsecus 32
*extroculare 44
*extrusare 45
*exturpare 44
*exturpidiare 44
f > sibilant 47
factum 86
*fao 18
fīgere 87
fistulare 86
fixare 86, 87
fixus 58, 87
flectere 29
*flecticare 30
*flescare 30
*fleskire 29
flexare 30
*flexicare 29, 30
flexus 29
fluxus, etc. 58
*frictiare 50
*furius 63
*gallius 63
-ges 38
Glaucus 62
*gredius 8, 9
*grevis 7
*grevius 7

hōc illi 47
hospitale 32
-iar 26
-iare 70, 81
-icare 37, 39, 49
-idiare 44
*impattiare 43, 67
impedicare 42, 43
impedire 67
-inare 87
*incalciare 70
*inconare 74
*infolliare 70
*infundiare 70
inquinare 74
*insulsicare 37, 39, 40
insulsus 37, 39, 40
-īscus 48, 49
-ittare 52
*jectare 55
*lascare 29
*lascus 75
laxare 38, 55
*laxicare 29, 75
laxus 75
*levius 7
luminare 61
*malatiare 25, 26
male luminatus 60
meare 15, 22
melancholia 74
migrare 65
miscitare 12, 24, 28
misculare 12, 28
-mn- 60
*mucceus 63
*muccius 63
*muccus 63, 66
*mukka 66
nans 18
nare 18
navigare 20, 22
-ncty- 56, 57
nervus 95
*nexicare 76
*notare 21
ordiniare 70, 81
*ordinium 81
*padium 50
pagensis 51
*pageus 51

WORD INDEX

*pagium 90
pagius 51
*patta 43, 67
pessulum 86
*physicar se 47
*pictare 57
*pinctiare 56
*pinctulare 55, 57
pingere 57
*pipa 84
plattus 36
*plattus 88
porrigere 51
*porro- iare 51
potionem 25
*pottarellu 66, 72
*pottarone 66, 72
*pottu 66, 72
*pottūrōne 72
*próbayo 18
propagare 38
quaerere 82
quassare 73
*quassiare 82
*questiare 82
radere 68
ramus 78
*rasclare 68
*rasicare 31
*rasiculare 68
*rasinare 87
*rasulare 68
rasurare 68
*rebucinare 68
*recaptiare 75
*recognitiare 70, 71, 81
*recomputiare 69, 70, 80, 81
*redossiare 70
religāre 85, 87
renuntiare 68
*rictulare 85, 87
rĭgare 84
*rigulare 84
ringārī 85, 87
ringi 87
ringulare 87
rŏdere 31, 84
*rodiculare 84
*rosicare 31, 76
rosus 31
ruere 31

*ruspare 33
ruspari 33
*ruspicare 32, 33
s + l 68
saeta 42
sanctulum 55, 57
scapha 89
schidia 43
*schistiare 43, 44
sciscitari 78
sectus 87
*sedimen 35, 36, 39
separare 38
sēpo 89
*seritare 42
*sesecare 31, 32, 34, 35, 38, 76, 87
*sesecus 32
*sessicare 34, 37, 39, 87
*sexicare 35, 58, 87
*sexus 35, 87
*simare 36
*simatum 39
simus 39, 89
socerari 4
sordidus 41
*sphingula 17
spīcula 17
spinula 17
spīrare 86
*stao 18
stragare 34, 38
strages 34, 38
*stragicare 34, 38
strombus 89
stroppus 44
-sty- 36, 44, 63
*subsedicare 37
sŭcŭlus 79
suīllus 79
*sulsicare 39
suspicare 40
tabanus 84
tanare 53, 54
*taxitare 30, 31, 33
*topittare 52
torculum 44, 52
torpidus 44
torquere 74
*torticare 74
*tractiare 58
tremitare 12

tremulare 12
*tresaurus 52
*tropare 51
-tty- 68
turbare 51
*tūsare 79
tỹphus 89
ulucus 62
vado 21
*vannitare 16, 24
*vasium 41
vindicare 27

LYONESE

tona 84

PORTUGUESE

afagar 76
andar 22, 27, 28
atanar 54
azo 25, 26
bastar 17
boroa, etc. 86
correia 56
deitar 35, 58
deixar 55, 56, 58
despedir 55
despir 55
empachar 42, 67
espirrar 86
estropear 44
falquear 63
fechar 86, 87
fermar 86
geitar 55
lasca 74
lascar 74
leixar 58
louco 62
paspalho 87
pechar 86
quarquara 87
rego 84
rejeitar 55
*relhar 85, 87
rilhar 84, 85, 87
rosegar 76
rosnar 87
sestro 48
solho 79
tufo 89

PRE-ROMAN

*tauna 84

PROVENÇAL

aize, ais 25
anar 14, 16, 22, 27
avalir 64
basta 17
bastar 67
boutarel 66
boutareu 66, 72
empachar 42, 67
empedegar 42
escacha, etc. 30
escouicha 43
escouissa 43
esquéussa 43
esquinsa 43
esquissa 43, 44
malvaizar 26
poutaro 66, 72
quichà 50
rosegar 31
rozegar 76
souscà 39
tauna 84
touna Forésian 84
trobar 51
trolh 44
vandá 16

RAETIAN

ala 15, 22
amna 15
la 15, 22
ma 22
na 15, 22
sedim 39
spiout 84

RUMANIAN

amna 23
emna 22
îmbla 22, 25
imna 22, 23
împedicà 42
merg 22
părîngă 89

SANSKRIT

bahugú 93
çatagvín 93

WORD INDEX

gām 93
gāús 93
gā'vāu 93
gáve 93, 94
gó Prakrit 93
gó 93, 94, 95
góbhis 93
góbhyām 93
goṇa 93, 94
góṣ 93, 94
guṇá 93, 94, 95, 96
lokati 61
-na 94
rokati 61
saptágu 93
sarágh 95
sãraghá 95
snāvan 95
sugú 93

SARDINIAN

ispidu 84
konos 74
limaru 90

SPANISH

abarca 46
abarcar 46
-al 62
alarido 53
alucón 62
alumbrar 61
ancón 88
andar 22, 27, 28
atusar 79
b > g 68
baço O.S. 41
bastar 67
bastir 67
basto 67
bazo 41
becerro 42
beso 41
bis lumbre 61
cansar 73, 88
cedazo 42
cerdo 41
chista O.S. 78, 80
chistar 78, 80
chiste 78, 80
cimbre 35

cinchar 54
cincho 54
ciscar, ciscarse 47, 48, 49
cisco 47, 49
columbrar 60, 61
*columbre 60
consagrar 3, 4, 5, 6
consangrar 3, 6
consegrar 5
consograr 3, 4
consuegro 4
corcho 32
corral 62
*cuejar 83
*deexar 80
dejar 55, 58, 80, 87
derezar 58
despachar 43, 67
desquejar 43
destorgar 74
dexar O.S. 55, 56, 58, 80
empachar 41, 42, 67
esbroar 86
espeto 84
espiche 84
espita 84
espitar 84
esquejar 41, 43
esqueje 43
estorpar O.S. 44
estrogar 34, 38
*estrojar 45
estropear 41, 44
estrujar 41, 44
falagar O.S. 76
físico O.S. 47
halagar 76
-ido 53
laco 62
lancha 46
lasca 74
malvar, etc. O.S. 26
malvazo O.S. 26
mozo 63
nesga 76
ole 47
ordeñar 81
paloma 42
pinchar 51, 52, 55, 56
pintar 57
*queçar 82

quejar 87
quejarse 82, 83
quexar O.S. 82, 83
rajar 68
rasca 76
raxar O.S. 68
rebuznar 68
recamar 63
recontar 81
regazar 75
regunçerio O.S. 70
regunzar, regunçar 68, 69, 70, 80, 81
rematar 78, 79
rosca 29, 31
Sancho 55, 57
sesga 35
sesgar 31, 34, 35, 38, 87
sesgo 29, 31, 32
sija 36
sima 35, 36, 39, 74, 89
simado 35, 36, 39, 89

socarrar 77
sollo 79
sosegar 34, 37, 39, 40
soso 37, 39
sossacar 76
tábano 84
tio 41
topar 51
topetar 51, 52
tropezar 52
truja 44, 45
tufo 89
tusa 79
vendegar 34, 35
ventanal 62
vingar 27
vislumbrar 60, 61

SYRIAC

jrâdâ 10
pātūrtā 66, 72

www.ingramcontent.com/pod-product-compliance
Lightning Source LLC
Chambersburg PA
CBHW021845220426
43663CB00005B/411